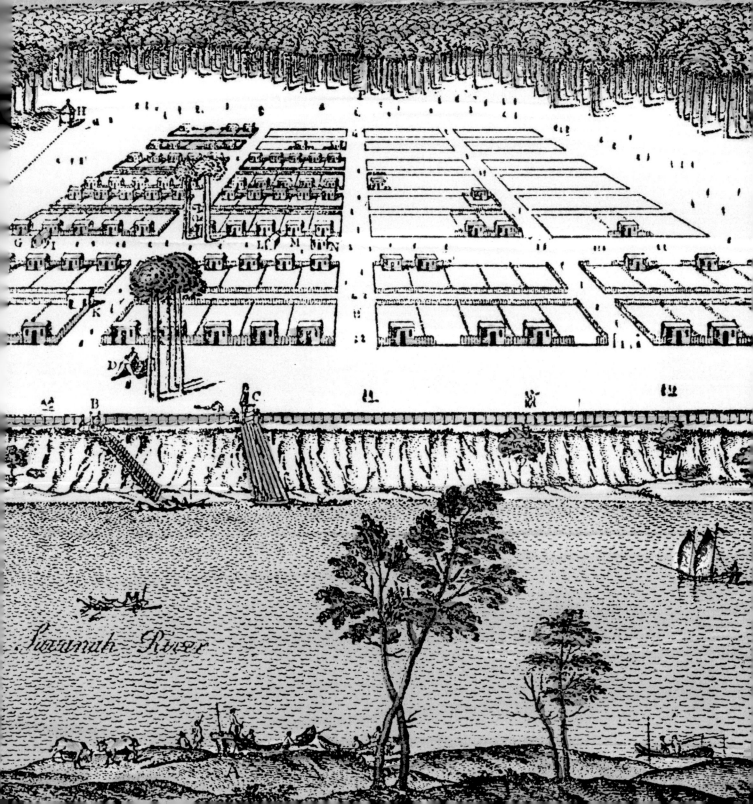

COLONIAL LIFE

Cities and Towns

Rebecca Stefoff

Sharpe Focus
an imprint of M.E. Sharpe, Inc.

Sharpe Focus
An imprint of M.E. Sharpe, Inc.
80 Business Park Drive
Armonk, NY 10504
www.mesharpe.com

ISBN: 978-0-7656-8109-6

Library of Congress Cataloging in-Publication Data

Stefoff, Rebecca,
  Cities and towns / Rebecca Stefoff.
      p. cm.–(Colonial life.)
  Includes bibliographical references and index.
  ISBN 978-0-7656-8109-6 (hardcover : alk. paper)
 1. Cities and towns–North America–History–17th century–Juvenile
literature. 2. Cities and towns–North America–History–18th
century–Juvenile literature. 3. Colonial cities–North America–Juvenile
literature. 4. City and town life–North America–History–Juvenile
literature. 5. North America–History–Colonial period, ca.
1600-1775–Juvenile literature. 6. United States–History–Colonial period,
ca. 1600-1775–Juvenile literature. I. Title.

HT122.S74 2008
307.76097–dc22

                                    2007007843

Editor: Peter Mavrikis
Program Coordinator: Cathleen Prisco
Production Manager: Laura Brengelman
Editorial Assistant: Alison Morretta
Design: Charles Davey LLC, Book Productions

Printed in Malaysia

9 8 7 6 5 4 3 2 1

Contents ❧

Located near the mouth of Virginia's broad and navigable James River, the English settlement at Jamestown was far enough inland to be sheltered from the most severe ocean storms, yet ships could easily reach the colonists.

CHAPTER ONE ⮑

From Camps to Communities

CHRISTOPHER COLUMBUS ARRIVED IN the Americas in 1492. When he sailed back to Spain, he left men behind to build a permanent settlement on the island of Hispaniola in the Caribbean Sea. That first attempt to create a European community in the Americas failed, as did some others. But before long the Spanish, and then other Europeans, managed to create lasting settlements in the Americas. Their towns and cities began appearing on maps of what they called "the New World."

Sometimes the Europeans simply took over an existing Native American city and made it their own. Tenochtitlán (teh-nohtch-tee-TLAN) was the capital of the Aztec Empire before the Spanish conquistador Hernán Cortés conquered it in the early sixteenth century, renamed it Mexico City, and made it the capital of what became a huge Spanish colony. More often, though, the English, Dutch, French, and Spanish settlers in the Americas built new towns and cities for themselves. These were small at first, often just a huddle of huts behind a wooden wall. But by the time the British colonies declared their independence in 1776, bringing the colonial period to an end with the birth of the United States, some of the settlements had grown into thriving towns and cities.

Urban centers in the American colonies, like cities and towns everywhere, existed on many levels. On the physical level, a city was made up of wood and stones and bricks, the materials that formed

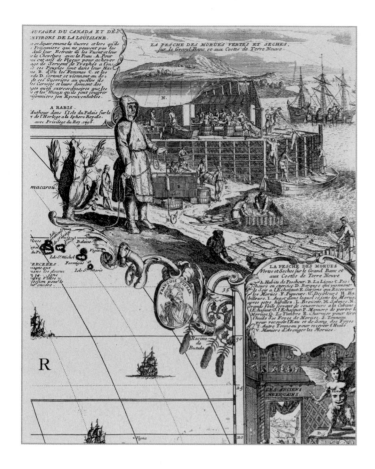

These scenes of fishing in North America are illustrations from a French map that was made during the colonial period. Fishing boats brought the catch to a camp on shore, where the fish was dried, salted, and packed in barrels to be shipped to Europe.

its houses, public buildings, and streets. Maps and drawings from colonial times, as well as written descriptions, give us some idea of the layout and physical appearance of cities and towns during the seventeenth and eighteenth centuries.

A colonial city or town also existed on the civic level, as a system of institutions that organized life for its inhabitants. Through these institutions, the people of the city governed themselves, traded, worked, worshipped, and pursued education and culture.

Finally, each city and town existed on the social level, as a community. On this level, a city was shaped by its people—their ethnic backgrounds, their social classes, and their ideas about how people should live. Some communities were highly homogeneous, meaning that most people came from the same background, shared the same religion, or were alike in other ways. Other communities were more heterogeneous, or mixed, with many different kinds of people. These varying elements were woven into the fabric of life in each city or town.

When people came from Europe or Africa to the colonies in North America, they brought with them the customs and traditions of their homelands. As they created new cities and towns in the colonies, they often tried to reproduce the familiar buildings, civic institutions, and community patterns of "the old country." Sometimes, they succeeded. Often, however, the new materials and living conditions that people encountered in the Americas led them to change their ways of doing things. Out of this mixture of old and new came colonial cities and towns that were distinctly American.

Fishing Camps

The first permanent English settlements in North America were Jamestown, established in Virginia in 1607, and Plymouth, founded by the Pilgrims in Massachusetts in 1620. Before those historic settlements came into existence, however, Europeans had made other landings along the Atlantic coast of North America. They had even created communities there. History books seldom mention these earlier communities. They were temporary, meaning they did not last very long, and some of them left no trace in the written records of their time. But the actions of the Europeans who spent time on North American shores before the founding of Jamestown and Plymouth had a lasting effect on the colonists who came later.

Fishermen from English ports such as Bristol, as well as from Portugal and other European countries, sailed far west into the Atlantic during the late fifteenth century. They were looking for fish, especially cod. They found vast quantities of cod and other fish in the banks, or areas of shallow water, off the coasts of present-day Maine and southeastern Canada. Fleets of fishing vessels sailed across the Atlantic, spent the summer months on the banks, loading their hulls with dried or salted fish, and returned to Europe at the end of the fishing season.

Historians know that just a few decades after Columbus's historic voyage, while European explorers such as Giovanni da Verrazano and Jacques Cartier were beginning the long process of mapping the Atlantic coast of North America, fishing crews were also landing on the

North American coast. They filled their ships' barrels with fresh water from rivers and streams, chopped trees into firewood so that they could smoke their catch over wood fires, and traded with the local Native Americans. Some historians have even suggested that a few of these fishing boats or fleets might have reached American shores before Columbus's historic voyage. If so, no evidence of their early landfalls has been discovered.

Archaeologists have found more than twenty sites along the Maine coast that Europeans used as seasonal or temporary fishing camps during the seventeenth century. They were using these sites at the same time as colonists were establishing the first permanent settlements that would grow into towns and cities. Researchers have unearthed relics left behind by the fishermen who made these early, unrecorded visits to America. Among the traces of their presence are broken clay pipes, buttons, and buried hoards of gold coins dating from the reign of Queen Elizabeth I of England (1558–1603).

First Communities

The first permanent English settlement in North America was established in 1607 at Jamestown, Virginia, far to the south of the Maine coast. It was founded as a moneymaking venture by a group of gentlemen, merchants, and adventurers who had organized themselves as the Virginia Company and received permission from King James I to set up a North American colony.

Yet in that same year, another group of English investors, also connected with the Virginia Company, tried to establish a settlement in Maine (which the English called "northern Virginia" at that time). Their fate shows the obstacles faced by those who tried to carve out the first European communities in North America.

The leader of the Maine colony was George Popham, the nephew of the Lord Chief Justice of England, who was one of the colony's financial backers. Second in command was Raleigh Gilbert, a relative of Sir Walter Raleigh, who was a well-known Elizabethan courtier and explorer.

Popham and Gilbert sailed from Plymouth, England, on May 31, 1607. Popham was in command of the *Gift of God*, while Gilbert's ship was the *Mary and John*. They took with them about 120 colonists. Their goal was to build a settlement where they could profit from the wealth they believed was waiting to be gathered in the Americas. They planned to get gold, silver, furs, and spices through trade with the Indians, but they also wanted to show that the forested American coast, with its plentiful supply of timber, would be a good site for a shipbuilding industry. Farmers, craftspeople, and shipbuilders were included among the colonists.

In August the two ships reached the Maine coast near the mouth of the Kennebec River. Popham and Gilbert chose a settlement site on a headland, a high point of land jutting out into the sea. There they began construction of an outpost they called Fort St. George. Like many other early settlements in the Americas, the Popham colony was first and foremost a fortress. Laid out according to the military principles of the time, the fort was designed to protect the colonists

The founding of Jamestown is idealized in this seventeenth-century illustration. At first, the settlement was entirely lacking in well-built structures, such as the building in the background.

The First Town Plan in the English Colonies ❧

One of the Englishmen who crossed the Atlantic with George Popham and Raleigh Gilbert was John Hunt. He was a draftsman—someone skilled in drawing plans and maps. On October 8, 1607, Hunt produced a map of Fort St. George, the fortress settlement built by English colonists on the coast of Maine. This map is considered the first town plan in the North American colonies, and one of the most detailed.

On Hunt's map, the outer wall of the fort is broken into a series of star-shaped projections. Military architects of the time favored this design, because cannons in the projections could be aimed in all directions to fire on an enemy approaching from any point. The map shows the position of nine guns along the wall. Inside the wall are residences for the colonists and for Popham, the "admiral," as well as public buildings: a guardhouse, a chapel, a workshop for barrel making, and a storehouse.

Just offshore floats the *Virginia*. Yet the ship had not yet been built by October 8, the date on the map. Either the drawing of the *Virginia* was added later, or Hunt placed it on the map in advance of its construction. Some historians have questioned whether the other structures on the map could have existed on October 8, less than two months from the time the colonists arrived. Perhaps Hunt's drawing was a plan for the settlement's future, not a map of how it really looked.

Between 1994 and 2005, an archaeological team excavated the site of Fort St. George. The researchers found traces of the "admiral's house," of a building where liquor was stored (probably for use in trading with the Indians), and of the general storehouse. Although their colony was short-lived, the first English settlers in Maine left evidence of their presence. Today the area is part of Popham Beach State Park.

from attack, whether by Indians or by hostile representatives of one of England's European enemies, such as Spain. The colonists would live and work in buildings inside the fortress wall.

The Pilgrims came ashore at Plymouth, Massachusetts, in 1620, weary of sea travel and grateful to reach land. After 1630, new arrivals from England swelled the Puritan ranks.

Popham and Gilbert also tried to establish trade with the Abenaki, the dominant Native American people of the area. They received a chilly reception, however. The Abenaki were mistrustful of the English, because earlier European visitors to the coast had kidnapped Indians to take back to Europe.

The colony had other problems, too. Provisions were short. The colonists had arrived too late in the season to grow any food for the winter. Half of them returned to England in the *Gift of God*. The others suffered through an unusually cold winter, during which a fire destroyed their storehouse and some of their scanty provisions. Rivalry broke out between Popham and Gilbert, with some of the colonists backing each of the two leaders. The rivalry ended when Popham died in February, leaving twenty-five-year-old Gilbert as the head of the colony.

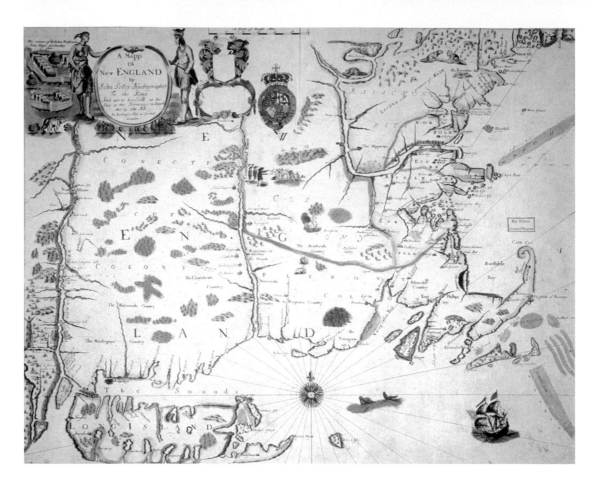

By 1675, when this map was made, English settlements had sprouted up along the east coast of North America. Virginia and Massachusetts were the most populated colonies.

The colonists did achieve some successes. Using timber made from local trees, they constructed a pinnace, or small ship, called the *Virginia*. It was the first vessel of its kind built by Europeans in North America. In time the Popham colony also managed to trade with the Abenaki for a cargo of sarsaparilla, a root used as flavoring and in medicinal tonics. Gilbert sent the sarsaparilla to England in the *Mary and John*.

When the ship returned, it brought news. Gilbert learned that his brother had died, leaving his title and his castle to Gilbert. The life of a pioneer on the rugged Maine coast lost its appeal at that point. Gilbert took the rest of the colonists back to England in the *Mary and John* and the *Virginia*, leaving Fort St. George to fall to ruin. The colony had lasted for about a year.

The end of the Popham colony did not bring an end to English settlement in North America, however. To the south, in Virginia, the colonists hung on at Jamestown, in spite of the fact that many of them died during the first few years from disease, starvation, and fighting with the local Native Americans. But the Jamestown colony endured this difficult period, which survivors remembered as the "starving time." Jamestown would become a profitable tobacco-growing settlement, the starting point for other settlements around the Chesapeake Bay, and, eventually, the capital of the Virginia colony.

English traders and colonists remained active, too, on the coasts of Maine and Massachusetts, despite the failure of the Popham colony and several other short-lived attempts at settlement. In the area that would come to be called New England, the English moved into Native American territory and created a network of settlements that sometimes cooperated and sometimes came into conflict.

Pilgrims, Puritans, and Native Americans

While tobacco-growing plantations took root in the area around Jamestown on the Chesapeake Bay, the next stage of English settlement on the northern part of the American coast was driven by religion. Protestant churches had come into existence in many parts of Europe during the sixteenth century, as people split away from the Roman Catholic Church to establish their own versions of Christianity. The Church of England, or Anglican Church, had been established as England's official Protestant faith, but some people were dissatisfied with it. They felt that it still contained too many elements of Catholicism. These people were called Dissenters, because they dissented, or disagreed, with the state church. Another name for

Metacom or Metacomet, known to the English as King Philip, was a son of Massasoit, the Native American chieftain of the Wampanoag people when the Pilgrims arrived. Later, during Metacom's time as leader of the Wampanoag, the Indians and the English fought in King Philip's War.

them was Puritans, because they wanted to purify, or reform, English Protestantism.

The Pilgrims were a group of Puritans who set out for North America on what they considered a holy pilgrimage. They intended to build a new society, organized according to their beliefs. Their ship, the *Mayflower*, landed in 1620 at Plymouth Bay in what is now Massachusetts. The settlement that the Pilgrims founded there would become the first permanent English town in New England. Their experiences during the first year of settlement show some of the ways that Native American and European communities were interconnected in the colonies.

The Pilgrims found themselves on the New England shore, with winter approaching and food in desperately short supply. They survived only because they located some empty Indian houses, searched them for food, and found some stored grain. Still, their first winter brought terrible suffering—nearly half of the Pilgrims died.

The following spring, a Native American named Tisquantum (tih-SKWAN-toom), or Squanto, showed up at Plymouth. Tisquantum had been sent by Massasoit, the chieftain of the local Wampanoag tribe, to communicate with the Pilgrims. Tisquantum was able to communicate with them because he spoke English. Years earlier, he had been captured by the crew of a European ship and taken to Spain, from where he eventually made his way to England. An English ship had returned him to his homeland not long before the arrival of the Pilgrims. Tisquantum lived with the Pilgrims until his death in 1622.

The Pilgrims probably owed their survival to the Indians' grain and to Tisquantum's help—yet European influence on, or interference in, the Indians' lives, played a part as well. The Indians' houses and

This modern illustration shows the Pilgrims celebrating their arrival in America with a sermon. Despite its Puritan roots, Massachusetts would soon become home to many non–Puritan immigrants. The religious unity that the colony's founders had envisioned was never achieved.

their stores of grain were most likely available because their owners had died of a disease brought to the region by the European ships that visited the coast. As for Tisquantum, he owed his ability to talk to the Pilgrims to his being kidnapped and almost sold into slavery by Europeans.

The Pilgrims received help from another source, too. English fishing camps on the southern Maine coast, near the location of present-day Damariscotta, provided them with food at their time of greatest need.

Plymouth survived, and other settlements soon took root in Massachusetts. In the winter of 1623–1624, a group of English settlers tried to start a fishing colony near what is now Gloucester, Massachusetts. Some people from Plymouth joined them. The colony failed, and many of the colonists went back to England, but some of them moved to a new location called Naumkeag. They built a trading post and a small settlement there, and the site remained occupied, although the population was very small for the first few years.

In 1629 a group of English people, most of them Puritans, gained the right to colonize Massachusetts. They were organized as the Massachusetts Bay Company. Their fleet of eleven ships, carrying about 1,000 colonists with their livestock and tools, arrived in 1630 on the shores of Massachusetts Bay.

Over the next decade, about 20,000 more English colonists came to the Massachusetts Bay. Some of the Puritans settled in Naumkeag, which was renamed Salem in 1629. Others founded Boston, Rockport, and other communities around the bay. Although only about half of the Massachusetts colonists were Puritans, the Puritans controlled the colony for some time, because only male church members could vote and hold office in local government.

"The Very Scumme of the Earth"

The Puritans hoped to build what they called "a city on a hill"—a religious colony that would be strictly governed by the principles of their faith. Although they sought the freedom to practice their religion on their own terms, they did not always grant the same freedom to others. The fishing camps and communities that continued to exist along the coast, in places such as Richmond Island in Maine and Nantucket and Marblehead in Massachusetts, were a constant source of irritation to Puritan leaders.

These fishing communities were informal and non-Puritan. Some, such as Richmond Island, favored the Anglican Church's version of Protestantism over that of the Puritans. The Massachusetts Puritans disapproved of the social and religious practices of the fishing communities, such as feasting, rather than fasting, during Christmas and other holidays. In addition, the fishing colonies tended to be more multicultural and multiethnic than the Puritan-dominated settlements. English people lived and worked alongside folk from Wales, Ireland, and the French-speaking islands of the English Channel. According to the Puritans, the men and women who lived in these settlements were a rough, disorderly lot, given to swearing and to what the Puritans considered an immoral way of life. John Winthrop, the governor of the Massachusetts Bay Colony, called the people of the neighboring fishing communities "a multitude of rude and misgoverned persons, the very scumme of the earth."

Massachusetts Puritans cast a cold eye on Thomas Morton's nearby settlement of Merrymount, or Ma-re-mount, where such frolics as maypole dancing took place.

The Puritans had the same low opinion of independent-minded colonists such as Thomas Morton, who became a big problem for them. Morton was an English lawyer who had come to Massachusetts years before the big Puritan migration started. Morton had arrived in 1624 with a group of colonists. They built a settlement about 30 miles (48 kilometers) from Plymouth and called it Ma-re-mount, or Merrymount. It included a plantation on which settlers could grow food and a trading post where they could obtain furs from the Native Americans in the area.

Merrymount prospered, which may have frustrated the Pilgrims, who were barely getting by at Plymouth. Morton and his companions also angered the Pilgrims—and later the other Puritans who settled in the Massachusetts Bay Colony—by their lively way of life. The Puritans were especially offended when Morton and the others at Merrymount set up a maypole and invited the natives to join them in

Life and Death Among the Indians ❧

In his book *New English Canaan*, published in 1637, colonist Thomas Morton described his feud with the Puritans of the Massachusetts Bay Company. He was sharply critical of their practices, and he moved to Maine after years of conflict with their leaders. In his book, Morton also described the customs of the Native Americans, for whom he had respect and affection. One section of the book praises the Indians' generosity and hospitality:

> [T]hey are willing that any shall eat with them. Nay, if any one that shall come into their houses and there fall a sleepe, when they see him disposed to lie downe, they will spread a matt for him of their owne accord, and lay a roll of skinnes for a boulster [pillow], and let him lie. If he sleepe untill their meate be dished up, they will set a wooden bowl of meate by him that sleepeth, and wake him saying, Cattup keene Meckin: *That is, If you be hungry, there is meat for you, where if you will eat you may. Such is their Humanity.*

Morton also tells how, before the Pilgrims arrived to begin the settlement at Plymouth, a French ship visited Massachusetts Bay. When a fight broke out between the Indians and the French, the Indians captured some Frenchmen and kept them as slaves. Soon afterward, Morton says, the Indians fell victim to an epidemic of disease that had been carried by the Europeans:

> [I]n short time after the hand of God fell heavily upon them, with such a mortal stroke that they died on heaps as they lay in their houses; and the living, that were able to shift for themselves, would run away and let them die, and let their carcasses lie above the ground without burial. For in a place where many inhabited, there hath been but one left alive to tell what became of the rest; the living being (as it seems) not able to bury the dead, they were left for Crows, Kites and vermin to pray upon. And the bones and skulls upon the severall places of their habitations made such a spectacle after my coming into those parts, that, as I traveled in that Forrest near the Massachussets, it seemd to me a new found Golgotha [place of execution mentioned in the Bible].

dancing around it. This was a traditional pastime of the English countryside, but the Puritans considered the practice wicked and godless.

In 1628 the Puritans charged Morton with creating disturbances and selling guns to the Indians. They arrested him and sent him back to England for trial. Found not guilty, Morton returned to Massachusetts, where he discovered that the Puritans had cut down the Merrymount maypole.

A feud with the Puritans over trading rights led to Morton's second arrest. The Puritans burned down his house, seized his property, and packed him off to England again. There Morton wrote a book called *New English Canaan*, which contained some harsh words about the Puritans of Massachusetts and their leaders. He returned to the colony in 1643, only to be arrested once again, this time for stirring up people against the Massachusetts Bay Company. After spending a year in jail in Boston, and paying a substantial fine, Morton was released. He moved to Maine, the site of many "rude and misgoverned" fishing communities, and died there in 1647.

Plymouth is famous as the "first settlement" in New England, but it was not really the first, and it did not exist in isolation, alone on an empty American shore. Plymouth took shape alongside other English settlement sites, temporary or seasonal, along the coast from Massachusetts to Maine. In addition, Plymouth was deeply interconnected with the Native American communities of the area. The same was true of Jamestown in Virginia.

As people planned and built the first lasting communities in English North America, other enterprises and endeavors were going on around them, sometimes competing with them, sometimes supporting them. These links among communities remained in place throughout the colonial period, as the new towns and cities of North America grew in size and in number.

The port of Charles Town (later renamed Charleston) as it appeared around 1758. The city was the largest and busiest center of trade south of the Chesapeake Bay.

CHAPTER TWO ⁊

The Rise of Cities in the British Colonies

PEOPLE FROM ENGLAND MADE THEIR first attempt to set up a colony in North America in 1584. Their colony was situated on Roanoke Island, Virginia. It failed, but the later settlement of Jamestown succeeded, as did Salem, Plymouth, and other settlements founded in the early seventeenth century. Still, in 1690, more than a century after the first settlement attempt, just five communities in the British colonies could be called cities—or even large towns.

The largest of these urban centers was Boston, with a population of 7,000. New York was second, with 4,000 inhabitants. Newport, Rhode Island, was occupied by 2,600 people. Philadelphia had 2,100 inhabitants, while Charles Town (later called Charleston), South Carolina, the biggest community in the southern colonies, had only 1,100.

Over the next eighty years, however, the population of the colonies grew rapidly. This growth was driven by immigration from the British Isles and from other European countries, as well as by the forced immigration of enslaved Africans. As the overall population of the colonies increased, its largest communities grew into substantial cities. By around 1770, a few years before the start of the American Revolution, Newport and Charles Town had more than 10,000 inhabitants each. Boston had 16,000 residents, and New York had 25,000. The largest city in the British colonies was Philadelphia, home to about 30,000 people.

Choosing a Site

The success of these cities was due, at least in part, to geography. When the first colonists arrived in North America to establish new settlements, they tried to choose sites carefully, with an eye toward permanent habitation. Even so, some colonial settlements were moved after the initial site proved unsatisfactory, or a better one was found.

What were the features of a good settlement site? The first arrivals looked for a number of things. Among the most important were accessibility, defensibility, and a good supply of drinking water.

Accessibility meant that the settlement was easy for ships to reach. Nearly all early settlements were located on the coast or a short distance inland on a river that flowed to the coast. An ideal site was either a sheltered bay, with water deep enough to serve as a harbor, or the bank of a navigable river that was deep and wide enough for ship traffic. Accessibility was important so that the colonists and their supplies could reach their settlement without much trouble. It was even more important, though, that the lumber, furs, or other goods that the colonists produced for export could easily be loaded onto outbound ships.

Defensibility meant that the settlement was easy to defend, or protect, from possible attackers. Many settlements began as forts, which were surrounded by protective palisades, or wooden walls. Certain geographical features, however, increased a site's defensibility. The planners who picked locations for settlements liked sites on peninsulas, coastal headlands, and tongues of land between two rivers, because such places were partly surrounded by water.

Water was important in another way when picking a settlement site: A settlement had to have access to fresh water. Although the European colonists collected rainwater in barrels and dug wells to tap into groundwater, the easiest way to get water was to take it from a

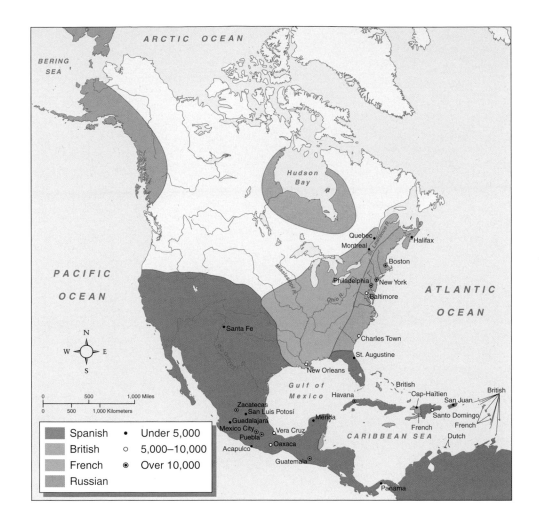

By the middle of the eighteenth century, four European powers had laid claim to parts of North America. Spain's Mexico colony had a number of good–sized cities, and English North America had three: Boston, New York, and Philadelphia. Europeans had barely made a mark on the vast interior of the continent.

nearby river, stream, or spring. Most settlements were located on or close to such water sources. Some communities benefited by having fast-running streams that could be used to turn waterwheels, driving sawmills and flour mills.

Another feature that contributed to a settlement's long-term prosperity was closeness to good agricultural land. The colonies had to produce enough food to feed their own people and a surplus to sell for export. It was necessary for the colonists to have something to export so that they could make money to buy the things that, at first, they could not produce locally—things such as glass, paper, and other manufactured goods.

This 1777 map of New York was based on a survey made just before the start of the Revolutionary War. Open, forested land and hills were still very much a part of New York's landscape.

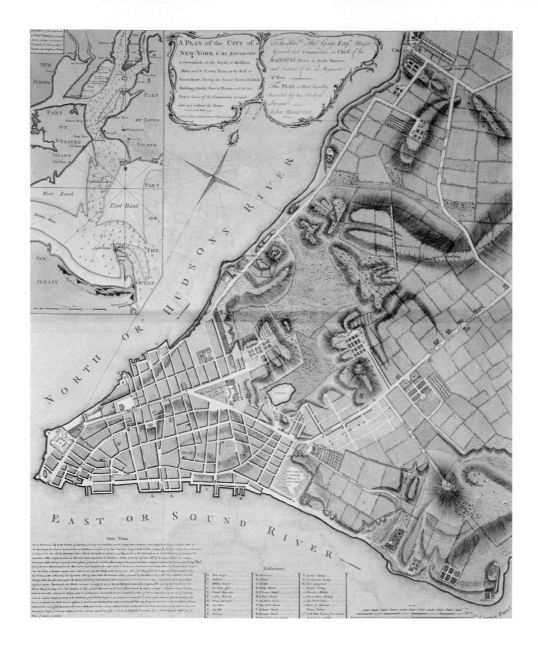

Settlements that were located in or near such productive agricultural areas, with good harbors for shipping, thrived. One example is New Amsterdam, capital of the Dutch colony of New Netherland; it became the English city of New York in 1664. New Amsterdam had the best harbor in North America. It also sat at the mouth of the Hudson River, a waterway that connected the port with the rich agricultural estates that the Dutch colonists developed upriver, in the Hudson Valley. Boston is another example. It was situated at the mouth of the Charles River, a useful waterway, and its port was so well sheltered from the open sea that it could be used for most of the year, even during part of the winter. Newport was established in 1638 on another good year-round harbor, the best on Narragansett Bay.

But even though the colonial cities and towns had some things in common, they were also shaped by regional differences. The colonies of the Chesapeake Bay and the South had different kinds of settlers, with different goals, than did the New England colonies. Both the Chesapeake Bay and New England, in turn, were different from the Middle Atlantic colonies of New York, New Jersey, and Pennsylvania. The principal cities of each region reflected that region's underlying economic organization and its distinctive patterns of community.

Jamestown

The society that developed around the Chesapeake Bay—in Virginia, then Maryland, and then the northern part of North Carolina—had its start in a moneymaking venture funded by London merchants who provided the financial backing for Jamestown. That venture came close to collapsing in the early years, when Jamestown failed to produce a profit for its investors. Then colonist John Rolfe discovered that tobacco, a plant native to the Americas, grew well in the Chesapeake and could be sold for a high profit in England.

Rolfe's discovery saved the Virginia colony. It also set the pattern for future economic and social growth in the Chesapeake and the South. The colonies there would be plantation colonies, devoted to growing cash crops—first tobacco, then rice, indigo, and cotton—for export. The social order would be dominated by the gentry, an upper

Jamestown—the first permanent English colony in America—was burned by rebellious Virginians led by Nathaniel Bacon in 1676. The rebels were frontier and backwoods settlers who rose against the governor, because they felt he was not doing enough to protect them from the natives.

class that modeled itself on the English aristocracy and lived on large agricultural estates worked by laborers. At first, these laborers were indentured servants from England, who were free to farm for themselves after working for a set number of years to pay for their passage to America. By the 1680s, however, the Chesapeake planters had made the transition to using African slaves as laborers. By 1750, slaves made up two-fifths of the population in the Chesapeake. Small farmers, craftsmen, tradesmen, and poor white laborers occupied an uneasy social middle ground between the great planters on one side and the slaves on the other.

The economy of the region grew, and for a time Jamestown grew along with it. By 1640, it had more than 8,000 people, making it one of the largest population centers in the British colonies. It had a brick church and was Virginia's capital. Jamestown could have gone on to become one of the most important cities in early America, but events in the 1660s and 1670s turned the city in a different direction.

One of these events was an economic slump. Ever since the founding of the colony, all traffic into Virginia had been required to go through Jamestown. This was good for the inns, shops, warehouses, and other businesses in the community. In 1662, however, the English crown ruled that other settlements could serve as ports of entry, and Jamestown declined in importance. A downturn in the price of tobacco also hurt the city's economy. The biggest, richest planters were able to hold onto their power and property, but it became harder for small planters to make a profit or to move up in the colony's social and political network.

Another blow fell in September 1676, when a rebellious colonist named Nathaniel Bacon, angry at some of the decisions made by Sir William Berkeley, the colony's governor, marched his followers to the capital and set it on fire. Jamestown was destroyed. Rebuilding took place, but it did not restore the community to its former importance. In 1699 Virginians relocated the colony's capital to Williamsburg, a town farther inland, on the James River.

Charles Town

Carolina, the colony just south of Virginia, was founded in 1670 by a group of English planters. About half of them came from the colony of Barbados, an island in the Caribbean that was one of the most profitable properties in England's empire, thanks to its sugar

A Storm Strikes Charles Town ♋

"Charleston is cursed with water," writes historian David S. Shields of the University of South Carolina. During the colonial period, the city, which was then known as Charles Town, had water in its streets during heavy rains and unusually high tides. The hurricanes that raged along the coast also brought floods, along with gales of wind. Four of these fierce storms descended upon Charles Town between 1700 and 1752. The devastation brought by the 1752 hurricane was described in the *South Carolina Gazette* of September 13 of that year—in images that might seem familiar to modern viewers who have watched television coverage of recent hurricanes on the American coast:

> *All the wharfs and bridges were ruined, and every house, store, &c. upon them, beaten down, and carried away [with all the goods, &c. therein], as were also many houses in the town; and abundance of roofs, chimneys, &c almost all the tiled or slated houses, were uncovered; and great quantities of merchandize, &c in the stores on the Bay–street, damaged, by their doors being burst open: The town was likewise overflowed, the tide or sea having rose upwards of Ten feet above the high–water mark at spring tides, and nothing was now to be seen but ruins of houses, canows [canoes], wreck of . . . boats, masts, yards, incredible quantities of all sorts of timber, barrels, staves, shingles, household and other goods, floating and drive[n], with great violence, thro the streets, and round about the town.*

plantations, which were worked by African slaves. The colony's owners were a handful of English noblemen to whom King Charles II had granted the right to develop Carolina. They planned an orderly colony with settlers concentrated in towns so that they could be easily governed. Instead, the settlers who went to Carolina quickly bought from the colony's land dealers as much property as they could get along rivers, stubbornly spreading out onto individual plantations, rather than forming the tidy towns that the owners had envisioned.

There was, however, one good-sized settlement in Carolina. After 1691, when Carolina was divided into northern and southern colonies, that city was the largest urban center not just in South Carolina but in all of the southern colonies. It was Charles Town, named for the king.

The founders originally established Charles Town in 1670 on the south side of a river that flowed into a bay. After the first ten years, however, the colony's proprietors, or owners, moved the town across the river. The new site was a peninsula between two rivers, the Ashley and the Cooper. (The rivers' names are a reminder that many landmarks in and around colonial cities bear the names of people who played a role in founding the settlements—people such as Anthony Ashley Cooper, one of the proprietors of Carolina.)

The city that rose on the new site was built according to a plan. Urban planning was one of the most distinctive features of colonial

Tobacco was the key to prosperity for settlers who lived around the Chesapeake. The best place to grow tobacco was along rivers, as the crop could be easily loaded onto the trade ships.

towns and cities. Most European cities were old. They had developed over long periods of time, as ancient or medieval communities expanded with the centuries. Their streets, often narrow and winding, did not follow any orderly pattern. If part of a city was leveled by fire, such as the Great Fire of London in 1666, the authorities might take advantage of the event to rebuild the burned part of town in a more modern manner, with wider streets arranged in a grid, or pattern of squares. Creating a brand-new settlement in North America was a chance to build a model modern city from the ground up. Some of the people who founded colonies or settlements spent considerable time and energy developing plans for what they hoped would be perfectly organized communities.

In the case of Charles Town, the model community would consist of a port, a fort, and a town. The port was the edge of the city on the Cooper River, with a broad street, or thoroughfare, running along the water's edge. The fort was considered necessary not just for protection from possibly hostile Indians but also because the settlement was close to Spanish territory in Florida. For protection, the founders of Charles Town built a wall that enclosed the city. Most of it was made of piled and packed earth, but some sections, such as the watch towers, were made of brick. Inside the wall was the city itself—337 numbered lots crisscrossed by a grid of streets.

The streets were not given official names, so one feature of colonial life in Charles Town was confusion over directions and addresses. People used informal names that changed often. Sometimes they used different names for the same street. One stretch of street, for example, was known as Middle Street by many people, but some called it Poinsette's Alley after a well-known local landmark, Poinsette's Tavern. Not until the 1730s did the colonial legislature start passing laws to give permanent names to the city's streets. One typical law, passed

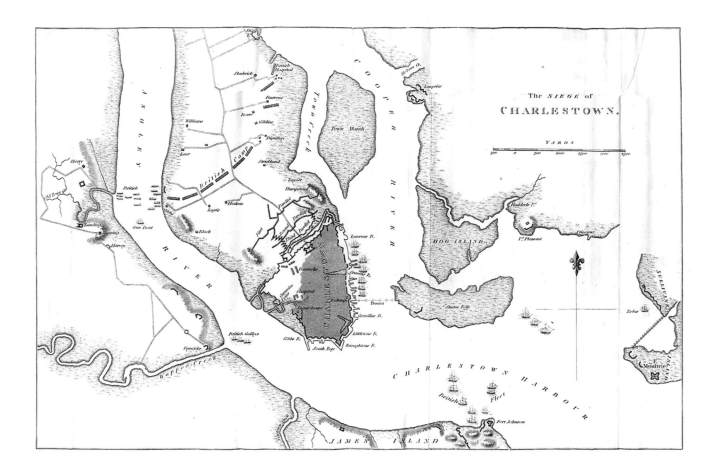

The SIEGE of CHARLESTOWN.

in 1734, required "That the said Street formerly known by the Name of Dock-street, shall for ever hereafter be call'd and known by the Name of Queen-street."

A man named Timothy Ford, who moved from Philadelphia to Charles Town in the eighteenth century, noticed at once how quiet the city was. In most colonial cities, the streets were paved with cobblestones. These round, closely packed stones created a firm surface but caused considerable noise when horses' hoofs and wagon or carriage wheels clattered over them. In Charles Town, though, the streets were simply paths of sand. Occasionally the city commissioners would release drunken sailors and other inhabitants of the town jails and direct them to rake the streets clean. The main problem with the unpaved streets was that when the sand was soaked with rainwater or

During the Revolutionary War, the British attacked Charles Town (later known as Charleston), South Carolina. This map from the period shows the British fleet in the harbor and the British camp, hospital, and siege lines north of the city.

floodwater, wagons could not travel over the streets. Their wheels became mired down in the wet sand.

Charles Town endured three crises in the mid-eighteenth century. In 1739 the city was shocked and terrified by the Stono Rebellion, a slave uprising that was quickly and severely crushed. The following year a huge fire destroyed much of the city. Some white residents believed that blacks had set the fire, but its origin is not known for certain. Just two years later, while the people of Charles Town were still rebuilding their city, a Spanish force landed on the coast south of Charles Town and threatened to advance on the city. The attack never came, and the threat faded.

The rebuilding continued, with new warehouses and grander homes replacing those that had burned. In 1800, Charles Town finally paved its streets, largely because of pressure from business owners and wagon drivers. By that time, the city was known as Charleston, a new form of its name that Americans adopted after the Revolution.

Boston

The most significant feature of settlement in New England was the Puritan influence. Although Puritans were not the only ones to settle in the region, they remained in political control of the Massachusetts Bay Colony for some time, and they had a strong effect on the development of city and town life throughout the area. Boston, the largest city in British North America during the seventeenth century, was their creation.

While John Winthrop and the Puritan emigrants were crossing the Atlantic in 1630, Winthrop preached a sermon to the other travelers on the ship *Arabella*. The sermon was titled "A Modell of Christian Charity." It used the metaphor of a "city upon a hill" to describe the

kind of community the Puritans would create in Massachusetts: an orderly, worshipful place that would stand apart from the rest of the sinful world but would serve as a model to show people how they could choose to live. The church would be the center of the community, just as religion would be the center of everyone's life. Inevitably, some members of the community would be better off than others, but Winthrop hoped that everyone would share and cooperate for the common good.

Winthrop and his followers landed first at Charlestown, in the Massachusetts colony, where a few English settlers were already liv-

During the eighteenth century, Boston saw a widening gap between the few rich people, who lived in fine mansions and prospered in shipbuilding and trade, and the growing number of poor people, who performed menial jobs or begged in the streets.

John Winthrop led a migration of about 700 Puritans to Massachusetts in 1630. They founded Boston as the seat of the colony's government. For most of the time from the colony's founding until his death in 1649, Winthrop served as its governor.

ing. As the colony's first governor, Winthrop had the authority to choose its place of settlement. Deciding that his community would need a better water supply than Charlestown offered, Winthrop relocated to a place already occupied by a settler named William Blaxton. The Puritans named this new site Boston, after an area in England where many of them had lived.

Cambridge and Charlestown were the other settlements nearby, and for a short time it was unclear which of them would be considered the colony's major city, or capital. By 1632, however, Boston had become the capital. Winthrop's metaphor of the city on the hill became reality there, but neither the city nor the Puritan commonwealth around it turned out exactly as Winthrop had hoped.

For one thing, the Puritans had planned to become farmers in Massachusetts, but they discovered that the region's rocky soil and its short growing season meant that they could not grow plantation crops such as tobacco and rice, the economic mainstays of the Virginia colony. They could grow other food crops, and they found the area good for grazing cattle, so they were able to feed themselves and even to export some food products, such as grain, preserved beef, and butter. Almost at once, however, many Puritans turned to the sea as the basis of their livelihood.

Some fished. Others took to waterborne trade, using small boats to carry goods to and from the English settlements and Native American communities around Massachusetts Bay, and beyond. Trade became the backbone of Boston's economy. As early as 1631 Bostonians had established commerce with the Virginia colony, exchanging barrels of salted northern cod for bushels of southern grain. By the end of the 1640s Boston's trade network had reached out to include English colonies up and down the Atlantic coast, the Dutch colony in New York, and the French colony in Canada. And during the 1660s Boston's traders ventured to more distant ports in the Caribbean, Europe, and Africa. The merchants of the city became heavily involved in a cycle of commerce that later historians called the "triangle trade." It involved slaves from Africa, sugar from Barbados and other Caribbean plantation colonies, and molasses and rum, which were manufactured in New England from the imported sugar.

Along with trade rose the shipbuilding industry. The first large vessel manufactured in Massachusetts was the *Blessing of the Bay*, launched at the mouth of the Mystic River in 1631. Within twenty-five years, shipwrights around the Mystic River and in other locations near Boston had built about 300 oceangoing ships and more than 1,000 smaller boats for local fishing and trade.

Boston quickly became a commercial city, where the possibilities of profit and individual enrichment sometimes clashed with the religious and civic ideals of Winthrop and the other Puritan founders. Many of those who were attracted to the city by its economic prospects were not Puritans, and gradually the Puritans' hold on the city waned.

Unlike many cities and towns in the American colonies, Boston took shape without a formal urban plan. Instead, it developed as a tangle of narrow streets that wound around hills and the Common, an open area in the center of town. In the mid-eighteenth century, Boston had seventeen churches. Most were Congregational, the church of the Puritans, but other faiths were represented as well. The city also had a meetinghouse, a state house that served as the seat of government, and Faneuil Hall, a large building given to the city by a merchant named Peter Faneuil in 1742 for use as a market. Although there were some buildings of brick and stone, many were still built of wood, which was plentiful in the region. Wooden structures burn easily, however, and Boston had five bad fires between 1670 and 1760.

One significant feature of Boston's city life during the eighteenth century was the widening gap between rich and poor. By 1770, half of all the wealth in the city was in the hands of just 5 percent of its population. The richest merchants lived in large, costly mansions on King Street, in the exclusive part of town called the North End. They rode in carriages, dressed in fine clothing imported from Europe, and employed large numbers of servants. At the same time, the number of poor people in Boston, and throughout New England, was growing. In 1757 Boston officials described "a great Number of Poor . . . who can scarcely procure from day to day daily bread for themselves & Families." Bostonians built workhouses, places where the poor could live and work to earn their keep, but the contrast between the city's haves and its have-nots created social tensions right up to the eve of the American Revolution.

Newport

Trade was also the lifeblood of New England's second-largest colonial city: Newport, Rhode Island. Newport had its origin in a religious dispute. In 1638 the Puritans expelled one of their group, Anne Hutchinson, from Massachusetts, because they thought her religious ideas were a dangerous departure from correct belief. She and her followers established a settlement called Portsmouth, at the north end of an island in Narragansett Bay.

The next year a split took place in their group. One member, William Coddington, led his own followers to the south end of the island, where they established Newport. With an excellent harbor, much closer to shipping routes than Portsmouth, Newport became a center of colonial trade and commerce.

Sandwiched between Boston to the north and New York to the south, Newport was not as large or influential as either of those cities during the eighteenth century. Still, it was a significant urban center. In 1731, nearly a century after its founding, Newport had 4,640 people and 400 houses, according to Rhode Island governor Joseph Jencks. That population would more than double in the next four decades.

Like Boston, Newport was connected to the world by shipping.

By about 1730, Newport, Rhode Island, had become a major trade port. Newport merchants were involved in the triangle trade of slaves (from Africa), sugar (from the Caribbean), and rum (made by American colonists from the sugar).

This illustration shows colonists cutting timber at a shipyard in Narragansett Bay. The plentiful supply of timber, including tall, straight pine trees for masts, made New England the colonial center of shipbuilding.

Merchants in Newport had links to others in London, the Netherlands, Charles Town in the Carolina colony, Barbados in the Caribbean, and West Africa. Newport was directly involved in the slave trade—ships owned by Newport merchants carried enslaved West Africans to markets in the Caribbean.

The city's most prosperous merchants, like those of Boston, built lavish mansions in the best neighborhood. In Newport's case, that neighborhood was the Point, which faced the harbor. Newport also had a government building, a large public square, and the Touro synagogue. Built in 1763, the synagogue is the oldest place of Jewish worship in America. It symbolizes one of Newport's most distinctive qualities: religious tolerance.

Puritan outcasts from Massachusetts, united by their passionately held beliefs, had founded Rhode Island and the city of Newport, but they permitted Quakers and others to live in the colony. More important was the fact that citizenship and participation in government were not limited to members of an official church, as they were in Massachusetts. In this sense Rhode Island was more egalitarian than was its parent colony. The Puritans of Massachusetts viewed Rhode Islanders with the same disdain they felt toward the unruly fishing communities of the northern coast. Bostonians sometimes called their neighboring colony "Rogue's Island," a reference to its supposedly sinful population.

The Touro Synagogue in Newport was the first place of Jewish worship in the colonies. Rhode Island was more tolerant of religious diversity than was its parent colony, Massachusetts.

In the middle of the eighteenth century, Britain and France went to war. The conflict was known in the American colonies as the French and Indian War. It hurt the economies of all the American cities that depended on international trade. Newport was smaller than the other major colonial ports, and it had fewer economic resources. Thus Newport suffered a decline and lost some of its importance.

A few years later, during the American Revolution, the British occupied Newport for several years. Many of the city's richest citizens fled the island. Although Newport never regained the commercial importance it had had during the colonial era, in the late nineteenth century it became a fashionable resort area for America's millionaires.

New York

New York, New Jersey, Pennsylvania, and Delaware were the Middle Atlantic colonies. Colonization in this region began not with the English but with the Dutch, who claimed territory in what is now New York. The Dutch colony, New Netherland, started out as an inland fort on the Hudson River, near the present-day location of Albany. The Dutch built the fort to trade with the Indians for furs, but they soon saw the agricultural potential of Manhattan, the neighboring Long Island, and the Hudson River valley. The Dutch West India Company, a trading firm, realized that New Netherland could produce food for the Dutch navy and merchant fleets, as well as for Dutch colonies in the Caribbean.

In 1625 the company founded a settlement at the southern tip of Manhattan Island. This outpost was meant to serve as a port and also to guard the approach to the Hudson River, the waterway to the company's inland fur trade. It was called New Amsterdam after the largest city in the Netherlands.

New Amsterdam became the chief port and commercial center of the colony, linking the agricultural estates along the Hudson with international trade. Yet the Dutch West India Company, busy with large-scale ventures in South America, Southeast Asia, and Africa, never made New Netherland a priority. New Amsterdam would not become a major colonial city until after the English took it over in 1664 and renamed it New York.

New York: A Stylish City ॐ

Sarah Kemble Knight, a widow who lived in Boston, was thirty-eight years old in 1704, when she traveled by horseback to the city of New York. Her account of the journey—complete with a frightening incident during which she was ferried across a flooded river in a canoe, and full of complaints about the terrible food she was served along the way—is a sharp-eyed (and sometimes sharp-tongued) description of life and travel in the American colonies at the beginning of the eighteenth century. When Knight finally reached New York, she was favorably impressed with the city's handsome buildings:

> The Cittie of New York is a pleasant, well compacted place, situated on a Commodius River wch [which] is a fine harbour for shipping. The Buildings Brick Generaly, very stately and high, though not altogether like ours in Boston. The Bricks in some of the Houses are of divers [various] Coullers and laid in Checkers, being glazed look very agreeable.

In Knight's time the European inhabitants of New York were still divided into English people and those of Dutch ancestry, who had come to the colony when it was still New Netherland. Knight has kind words for both the English and the Dutch New Yorkers, but her description of the Dutch women's bare ears (in the "French" style) and ornate jewelry seem to hint at Bostonian disapproval:

> [The people] are not strict in keeping the Sabbath as in Boston and other places where I had bin, But seem to deal with great exactness as farr as I see or Deall with. They are sociable to one another and Curteos [courteous] and Civill to strangers and fare well in their houses. The English go very fasheonable in their dress. But the Dutch, especially the middling sort, differ from our women, in their habitt go loose, were [wear] French muches wch are like a Capp and a head band in one, leaving their ears bare, which are sett out Wth Jewells of a large size and many in number. And their fingers hoop't with Rings, some with large stones in them of many Coullers as were their pendants in their ears, which You should see very old women wear as well as Young.

The Stadthuys in New Amsterdam (later New York) was the town hall of the Dutch colony from 1654 to 1699. Many buildings in New Amsterdam were built with stepped brick facings, a common architectural feature in the Netherlands.

One of the most notorious episodes in the city's early history took place the year after the Dutch West India Company founded it. In a transaction that was almost certainly understood differently by the two sides, officials of the company gave the local Native American people a small sum of money in exchange for Manhattan Island. It is most likely that the Indians, who did not share European ideas about permanent private ownership of land, believed that they had simply granted the Dutch the right to live on the land or use it for a period of time. The Dutch, however, considered that they had bought Manhattan, which from that time on was seen as European property.

Even though the Dutch were sure that they owned Manhattan, they did not do a great deal with it. In the first year of settlement, the colonists built a fort, thirty log houses, a trading post, and a mill that they also used as a church. Two years after its founding, New Amsterdam's population was only about 250.

The city's population remained small throughout the Dutch period. By 1664 there were only about 1,500 people living in and around New Amsterdam. They were clustered at the island's southern tip. Wharves ran along the western edge of the settlement, on the bank of the Hudson River. Behind them stood the square military fort. East of the fort were the streets and blocks of the town, including several large open spaces that were used as public squares. The northern boundary of the community was marked by a large protective wall that stretched across the island, separating New Amsterdam from the farms, pastures, and forests of central Manhattan. The street that ran along that wall is still known as Wall Street in modern-day New York City, and it has become the city's financial center.

New Amsterdam's population was never large, but it was always diverse. From early in its history the city was one of the most multicultural places in the colonies. This was partly because the Dutch people, by and large content in their homeland, were not particularly eager to emigrate to North America. Some Dutch families did come to New Amsterdam and New Netherland to work for the Dutch West India Company, but the company also recruited residents from among many ethnic and religious groups in northern Europe, especially those who were fleeing persecution in their homelands. Among them were Jews, Flemings and Walloons from present-day Belgium and northern France, Huguenots, Scandinavians, and Germans.

Black slaves were also part of New Amsterdam's multicultural mix. The company brought them to the colony from West Africa and the Caribbean. An African-Dutch culture emerged, in which black residents of New Amsterdam spoke Dutch, used Dutch names, and followed some European customs, while still retaining African traditions. Company practice allowed slaves to purchase "half freedom," a state in which they could marry, own property, and work for wages like other hired laborers or craftspeople. By 1664 New Amsterdam had about 300 African inhabitants. About one-fifth of them were free.

In 1653 New Amsterdam was formally incorporated as a city. A civic government was formed, made up of businessmen, community leaders, and property owners. They managed to win some control of local affairs from the strict rule of the company officials. The burghers, or burgomasters, as the new civic officials were called, deliberately emphasized the community's Dutch origins and identity. New tile-roofed houses were modeled on those of Amsterdam. To make New Amsterdam look more like old Amsterdam, which is built along a network of canals, the colonists surveyed and dug canals in their own city. Most significantly, they adopted the civic practices of the Netherlands, such as limiting the right to do business with people who owned property.

The burgher government of New Amsterdam seemed intent on strengthening the Dutch influence in the city. That changed, however, when English forces under the Duke of York gained control of New Netherland. In 1664 the colony became New York, and New Amsterdam became the city of New York.

During the remainder of the seventeenth century, French and

English immigrants came to the city, changing its ethnic and social mix. They also wrested control of the city's economic life from the Dutch, who still made up a majority of the white population.

The shift from Dutch to English control did not take place without upheaval. In 1689 a man named Jacob Leisler, representing a group of Dutch merchants in the city, rose to power in New York. Many of the area's Dutch residents backed Leisler, who encouraged them to believe that England would give up the colony. Two years later, however, the new monarchs of England, William and Mary, removed Leisler from his position in the city. The era of Dutch dominance was clearly over.

The city remained one of the most ethnically diverse places in North America, and it became one of the most religiously tolerant. Although the Dutch had allowed members of minority religions,

By 1768, when this church was built in New York, the former Dutch city had been in English hands for more than a century.

such as Quakers and Jews, to settle in New Amsterdam, they had not allowed them to conduct religious services. The English granted them that right. At the same time, the colony's leaders made aggressive efforts to bring both Dutch and French settlers into the Anglican church. To weaken the Dutch influence and promote the use of English as the primary language, the leaders prevented the Dutch Reformed Church from giving lessons to children for the first quarter of the century after the city became English.

Civic life in English New York moved in different directions for whites and blacks. Black residents of New York also lost some of the rights and freedoms they had had under the Dutch. A population of free blacks continued to be part of the city, although most of them lived on the farmlands north of the heavily settled district. The enslaved blacks worked chiefly as servants for the white residents. Slaves were treated more strictly than they had been under Dutch rule, especially after a slave revolt in 1712 and a series of fires, believed to have been set by slaves, in 1741.

New York grew in size and importance during the eighteenth century. Its harbor expanded until wharves lined both sides of southern Manhattan. Settlement advanced north of Wall Street along a wide thoroughfare known as the Broad Way. Today that street is New York City's famous Broadway, one of many distinguishing features of American cityscapes that date from the colonial era.

Philadelphia

The other major city of the Middle Atlantic colonies got a later start than did New York but grew more rapidly. By the end of the colonial period, Philadelphia was not just the biggest Middle Atlantic city but the largest city in British North America.

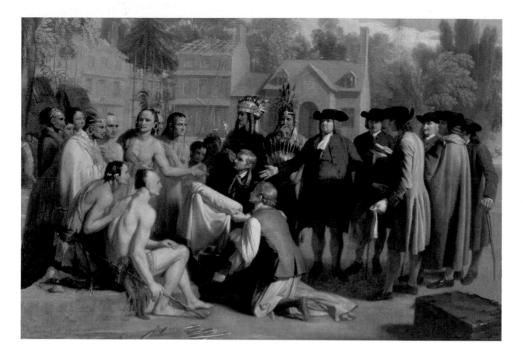

Here, William Penn and other leaders of the Pennsylvania colony arrange a treaty with the Lenni Lenape Indians. As a Quaker, Penn was opposed to violence and warfare, and he wanted his colony to be established on a peaceful footing.

Philadelphia was the creation of William Penn, an English Quaker, or member of the Society of Friends. In 1681 King Charles II repaid a debt to Penn's father by granting Penn a large colony in North America. Penn named the colony Pennsylvania ("Penn's woods") and chose the name Philadelphia for the capital he planned to build there. The name means "city of brotherly love." It reflects Penn's pious hope that the city would be a community governed by the Quaker virtues of peace, religious tolerance, charity, and neighborliness.

Penn encouraged people from Germany and France to settle in his colony, along with those who came from England, Scotland, Wales, and Ireland. At first he feared that the majority of emigrants to his colony would be farmers. While he knew that agriculture would play an important role in Pennsylvania, he was a city dweller who envisioned a city as a necessary part of a well-balanced colony. He was pleased that many who came to Pennsylvania were craftspeople and townspeople; instead of spreading out into the countryside on individual homesteads, as settlers in Carolina had done, these people wanted to participate in urban life. Penn had a city plan ready for them.

The British army is shown marching into Philadelphia during the Revolutionary War. Note the tower rising from the building now known as Independence Hall. This is where colonial leaders signed the Declaration of Independence.

Planning Philadelphia, in fact, was one of Penn's greatest pleasures when creating the colony. Penn had lived in London and Paris, centuries-old European cities where buildings crowded closely together along narrow, dark streets. He had seen how fires and plagues of contagious disease could sweep through such cities, and he was determined to design a city that would have urban advantages—such as diversity, economic opportunity, fellowship, and availability of education and culture—without the disadvantages of Europe's medieval cities. To achieve his vision, Penn had draftsmen draw up a city plan. Elements of the plan were later copied by the founders of many towns and cities across America.

The planners began with a location, a point of land where the Schuylkill River flows into the much larger Delaware River. Although this site was 100 miles (160 kilometers) from the sea, it was nevertheless a good port, because ships could sail up the broad and navigable Delaware River. Between the two rivers the planners laid out a grid of wide, straight streets running north to south and east to west. The plan included a large central square for the city hall, as well as other good-sized public squares, parks, and markets.

One of Penn's chief desires was to bring the healthful openness of country life into the city. He told the planners to make the house lots large enough for "Gardens or Orchards or fields, that [Philadelphia] might be a greene countrie towne, which will never be burned, and will always be wholesome."

Contrary to Penn's vision of harmony, Philadelphia was not free of conflict and controversy. Penn himself was involved in a long dispute with some of the colonists who bought the first town lots. As proprietor of the colony, he angered some of the colonists who disagreed with his decisions, such as his insistence that they provide him with an income and that they, not he, pay certain fees owed to the crown. But after about 1701, when Penn left the colony for England, never to return, the people of Pennsylvania, especially the Philadelphians, gradually claimed more and more control over their government.

Philadelphia, like Boston and New York, was built upon trade. It was the port of entry for manufactured goods from European ports that were sold to colonists throughout the Delaware River valley and beyond. It was also the place where cargoes of grain, preserved meat, and leather, the products of the rich agricultural lands in the colonies of Pennsylvania, New Jersey, and Delaware, were stored and loaded aboard ships for export. Philadelphia was home to many businesses that catered to the warehousing and shipping trades: barrel makers, wagon drivers, and sellers of ship's supplies such as rope and canvas.

By the eve of the American Revolution, Philadelphia was recognized as a leading center of commerce, education, and political thought. Centrally located between the southern and northern colonies, the city was a natural choice for the informal capital of the rebellious colonies when they began to organize themselves to resist British rule.

The majority of colonial Americans lived in rural homes, not in the cities, although most lived in smaller and humbler settings than this manor house on a Maryland plantation.

CHAPTER THREE ❧
Towns and Villages

BOSTON, CHARLES TOWN, NEWPORT,

New York, and Philadelphia were the major cities of the British colonies in North America, but smaller cities and towns also were found in the colonies, especially during the eighteenth century. These communities, like the bigger cities, were hubs of trade and commerce for the people who lived in the surrounding countryside.

Most people *did* live in the countryside during the colonial period. As much as 95 percent of the colonial population lived in rural settings, not urban ones. But although many of the people who came to America were drawn by the lure of owning their own farmland, some settlers and immigrants wanted urban lives. They created the cities and towns that increasingly dotted the landscape. Beyond the cities and towns, a growing number of smaller villages and hamlets became centers of community life for the Americans who lived on individual, widely scattered farms and homesteads in the final decades of the colonial period.

Smaller Cities and Towns

Throughout the eighteenth century, Charles Town was the largest and most important colonial city in the southern colonies. During the middle of the century, however, another community on the southern coast rose in importance: Savannah, Georgia, just across the border from South Carolina.

Savannah was a carefully planned city. James Oglethorpe, the founder of the Georgia colony, chose its location: the top of a bluff next to the Savannah River, a few miles inland from the coast, with room for as many as 400 ships to dock at the same time. Oglethorpe also laid out the city plan. Savannah would be organized into a set of wards, or neighborhoods. Each ward had forty lots arranged around a good-sized public square. Throughout the colonial period these public squares served several purposes. They were open-air market-places, public meeting places, and places for people from outlying settlements and farms to gather in times of danger. Today they are regarded as one of Savannah's most recognizable and attractive features—another legacy from the builders of colonial towns.

The settlement was founded in 1733 with 114 residents. In the shadow of the more established, prosperous urban center of Charles Town, not far to the north, Savannah grew slowly. By 1760 it was still nothing more than a couple hundred wooden buildings. It had no structures of brick or stone—the kind of buildings that were mile-stones in colonial communities, because they represented wealth and permanence. The following year, only forty-one ships entered the town's harbor.

Things picked up for Savannah during the 1760s, however. Rice became a major crop in South Carolina, and port activity increased. In 1763 publication of the colony's first regular newspaper, the *Georgia Gazette*, began in Savannah. By 1771 the number of ships entering the harbor had risen to 217. And in the mid-1770s, just before the Revolutionary War, Savannah's population was about 3,500, making it the second-largest city in the southern colonies, after Charles Town.

Another important southern town was Williamsburg, which replaced Jamestown as the capital of Virginia in 1699. Williamsburg was founded in 1650 by John Page, a British planter who spent his

The Savannah River

life—and a considerable sum of money—boosting the fortunes of the settlement. He donated land for one of the town's biggest churches and served in the colonial government. Page also helped establish the College of William and Mary, the second-oldest college in the colonies after Harvard, which was founded in Cambridge, Massachusetts, in 1636. William and Mary's first building, designed by well-known British architect Christopher Wren, was completed in 1699. Finally, it was Page who convinced the colonial government to relocate to Williamsburg after Jamestown burned in Bacon's Rebellion of 1676.

Williamsburg was the site of the first theater in the colonies, built in 1716. It also had the House of Burgesses, where the colonial legislature met, and a stately residence for the governor. Williamsburg was a stylish, cultured city, but it remained small. In 1750 it had only about 3,000 inhabitants and 300 homes—although the city's popula-

Savannah, Georgia, was a planned city with an urban landscape organized around open squares. By the time of the American Revolution, it had become the second-largest city in the southern colonies.

The first building at William and Mary College in Williamsburg, Virginia, was completed in 1699. Today, it is the oldest academic building that has been continuously in use in the United States.

tion increased to almost 4,000 when the House of Burgesses was in session and the inns were full.

By and large, the residents of Williamsburg maintained a strongly English culture, and its leading citizens modeled themselves on the English gentry. Toward the end of the colonial era, as tension grew between the colonies and their parent country, many people in Williamsburg declared themselves loyal to the British crown.

Some colonial towns were settled by people who emigrated to America as a group and tried to recreate the conditions of their homeland. One example of this kind of homogenous settlement is New Bern, North Carolina. It was founded in 1710 by Baron Christophe von Graffenried, a nobleman who led a group of settlers from Switzerland and a neighboring region of Germany called the Palatinate. They founded a port town that they named after Bern, the Swiss capital. Between 1770 and 1792 New Bern served as the capital of North Carolina. As a port town, New Bern's chief business was the export of forestry products used in the shipbuilding and construction industries, such as tar and shingles, made from the region's pine forests.

Baltimore, Maryland, was an important large town—or small city—by the end of the colonial period, although it got a late, slow start. In 1729 the government of the Maryland colony assigned some commissioners to buy land near the head of Chesapeake Bay and establish a city that would be called Baltimore. The commissioners bought up three small settlements. One of them, Baltimore Town, became the center of the new city.

At first, Baltimore consisted of just sixty lots of one acre each. A settler could buy only one lot and had to build on it within eighteen months. That rule was intended to keep people from turning the planned town site into a few large agricultural estates. The commissioners also hoped that this plan would stimulate rapid development.

The growth of Baltimore, however, was anything but rapid. For several decades the town was nothing more than a couple dozen houses, a church, a tavern, a brewery, a barbershop, and a shed for inspecting tobacco crops. During the 1760s, though, Baltimore's port came into greater use by both local and international shipping companies. It became a major exit port for the wheat, corn, tobacco, and flour produced in the area. Expanding to swallow up two neighboring settlements, Baltimore had a population of almost 7,000 by the

Court House Square, in Salem, Massachusetts, illustrates a key feature of many colonial towns: a central square with important public buildings set around it.

start of the American Revolution, making it the largest town in the Maryland colony.

Just off the northern coast of Maine is the island of Nova Scotia. In the seventeenth century the French claimed Nova Scotia as part of their colony along the St. Lawrence River. A treaty made in Europe in 1713, however, gave ownership of Nova Scotia to Great Britain, even though some French settlers already occupied the island.

Nova Scotia was a sore point between Britain and France. The French were nervous about having the British on Nova Scotia, because the island guards one side of the entry to the St. Lawrence, France's vital waterway into its colony. Britain, in turn, felt uneasy about being so close to the French, who built a massive military fort called Louisbourg on a nearby island and who tried to invade Nova Scotia in 1746. To reinforce their control, the British decided to establish new settlements on the island. One of them, Halifax, was located on a large harbor. It became the northernmost town in a string of ports along the New England coastline.

The slave trade contributed to the growth of the American colonies. Northern merchants profited from the shipping of slaves, while the labor of slaves fueled the rise of a plantation economy in the southern colonies.

Halifax was originally called Chibouctou (shee-BOOCK-too), the French version of its Native American name. When 2,500 British settlers arrived in 1749, the name was changed to Halifax. The settlers, a mixture of former soldiers and craftspeople such as carpenters, built a heavily fortified settlement that featured a wooden palisade, five forts, and three sets of cannon.

The commander of Halifax, a British army officer named Edward

Cornwallis, made no attempt to form good relations with the local Indians—in fact, he treated them with contempt and hostility. The Indians returned the hostility and, as a result, the English colonists were more or less confined to the town, or to nearby areas that could be defended from the forts. After Cornwallis left Halifax in 1752, some of the settlers moved south to New England. At the same time, some New England businessmen moved north to Halifax, sensing good business opportunities in a place where the government was spending money on defense.

In 1755, the English governor of Nova Scotia, fearing that the continued presence of the French settlers would lead to strife, ordered the French to leave the island. These Acadians, as they were called (from Acadia, the name they had given to their colony), were sent to other British colonies or to France. Some of the Acadians, however, resisted

Yale College was established in the Connecticut colony to teach religion, but it soon became known as a center of scientific study as well. Benjamin Franklin donated an electrical machine to the college.

A Plea to Tourists &

Michel Guillaume Jean de Crèvecoeur was born into the French nobility in 1735. At the age of twenty, this son of a count emigrated to New France, the French colony in Canada. He later moved to New York, became a citizen of that colony, and married a woman named Mehitable Tippet. Under the name John Hector St. John de Crèvecoeur, he later published a book called *Letters from an American Farmer* (1782) that gave European readers a look at life on the American colonial frontier. It also captured the independent, practical, and ambitious attitude that was coming to be thought of as the "American character."

In the first letter, or chapter, of his book, Crèvecoeur mentions the English love of traveling to see exotic places. But the lively new towns in America, he claims, are more worthy of interest than the ancient Roman ruins of Italy. Crèvecoeur's pride in the growing communities of his adopted country is clear:

Where is it that these English folks won't go? One who hath seen the factory of brimstone at Suvius, and town of Pompey under ground! [Mt. Vesuvius and the buried Roman town of Pompeii, in Italy] . . . We are all apt to love and admire exotics, tho' they may be often inferior to what we possess; and that is the reason I imagine why so many persons are continually going to visit Italy. That country is the daily resort of modern travellers . . . . There they amuse themselves in viewing the ruins of temples and other buildings which have very little affinity with those of the present age, and must therefore impart a knowledge which appears useless and trifling. I have often wondered that no skilful botanists or learned men should come over here [to America]; methinks there would be much more real satisfaction in observing among us, the humble rudiments and embryos of societies spreading every where, the recent foundation of our towns, and the settlements of so many rural districts. I am sure that the rapidity of their growth would be more pleasing.

the plans the British made for them; they made their own way to other parts of Canada and, eventually, to the colony of Louisiana.

Meanwhile, Halifax saw a boom in military industries, such as shipbuilding, during the French and Indian War, which began in 1754 and ended in 1763. As many as 22,000 soldiers and officers were stationed in the town, and overcrowding, drunkenness, and fighting became serious problems. After the war, however, the troops withdrew. Halifax resumed its normal size, with a population of about 3,700 people in 1767.

Ties of kinship and trade between Halifax and New England remained strong. At the time of the Revolutionary War, some residents of Halifax wanted to join the thirteen colonies in their rebellion against Britain. Leading merchants, however, believed that staying linked to Britain would be more profitable. In the end, Nova Scotia did not join the rebellion. Today it is part of Canada.

Villages and Rural Communities

Most of the colonies' proprietors and organizers wanted the colonists to settle in compact communities—in towns or, for rural residents, in villages or hamlets surrounded by farmland. That kind of concentrated settlement would make it easier for the colonists to defend themselves against Indians and other dangers. It would also make it easier for the authorities to keep track of, tax, and control the colonists.

The majority of colonists did not care about the proprietors' visions. They wanted to live on their own property and, if possible, to become farmers. This was the dream of a great many colonists who came to America from countries in which it had been impossible for them to own land. Everywhere in the British North American

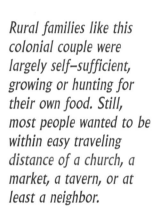

Rural families like this colonial couple were largely self–sufficient, growing or hunting for their own food. Still, most people wanted to be within easy traveling distance of a church, a market, a tavern, or at least a neighbor.

colonies, settlers spread out, claiming their own land and a chance to live in a household that was self-sufficient, or mostly self-sufficient. Very few of them, however, struck out for the remote frontier. Although they did not want to cluster in villages, they did want to have some contact with neighbors or perhaps a larger community, such as a fort or trading post.

The colonies filled with farmsteads that were separate, yet connected by footpaths, navigable streams, or, when the colonists had time to build them, wagon roads. During the seventeenth century, most people lived on farms within a comfortable traveling distance of other farms. Most of them could easily get to a town where church services, market days, and court sessions were held on certain days.

Even smaller villages also existed. From the earliest phases of colonial history, fishing communities such as Nantucket came together along the coast. The Puritans, who placed a high value on regular church attendance and participation in town meetings, also tended to form country communities that evolved into villages. In the rest of the colonies, villages and hamlets (even smaller rural communities) sprang up gradually.

During the eighteenth century, the population rose in almost all parts of the colonies. Settled areas became more densely inhabited. This increase in population pushed the frontier of settlement westward, but it also created a network of small urban centers in what had once been rural landscapes. These communities were especially likely to form in places with highly productive agriculture or industries, such as shipbuilding or leather making, or at favorable transportation points, such as the crossing of two main roads or the junction of two rivers.

Even the smallest hamlets and villages typically had a church, a tavern, and a store. Larger villages and towns had two or three of each, along with an inn at which travelers could stay, and probably the workshops of craftsmen such as woodworkers and blacksmiths. The populations of these settlements might never have risen above a few hundred during the colonial era, but they stitched together the scattered rural population, providing opportunities for people to socialize, hear the news, and take part in the regional trade network by selling their produce and buying necessary goods. The interactions that occurred in the small towns and villages made country-dwelling colonists feel connected to the larger colonial world.

Throughout the eighteenth century, clusters of homesteads slowly grew into hamlets, then villages. Some of the villages eventually became small towns. This type of landscape was more familiar than the big city to many colonial Americans.

Montreal was France's gateway to trade and exploration in the North American interior. For years, the settlement prospered from the fur trade, which was France's principal economic activity in Canada.

CHAPTER FOUR ❧
Spanish and French Colonial Cities and Towns

THE COLONIES THAT BRITAIN ESTABLISHED along the Atlantic coast of North America were small compared with the vast tracts of territory claimed by Spain in Florida and the Southwest, or those claimed by France in Canada and the Mississippi River valley. Although the British colonies were smaller in area than the Spanish and French colonies, they had many more inhabitants. In Spanish and French North America, fewer people were distributed thinly across far greater areas.

Nevertheless, towns and cities emerged in Spanish and French territory. These communities were shaped by the colonial policies of their parent countries, as well as by the customs of the people who settled them. Traces of those policies and customs still can be seen in the architecture and history of some modern cities in the United States and Canada.

Civic Life in the Spanish Borderlands

Spain's chief interests in the Americas were in the Caribbean, Mexico, and Central and South America, where its largest, most profitable colonies were located. Spain did, however, colonize two parts of what is now the United States. Spanish colonies in Florida and in the Southwest were natural extensions of Spain's holdings in the Caribbean and in Mexico. Because Florida and the Southwest formed the northern edge of Spanish territory, this region came to be called the Spanish Borderlands.

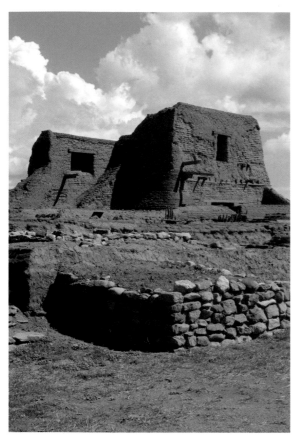

Once centers of Spanish colonial rule in New Mexico, this and most other Spanish missions are now in ruins. Spain's attempt to extend its colony north into New Mexico met with resistance from the Native Americans in the area.

The Spanish originally explored the Borderlands looking for gold and silver, or other sources of wealth. They did not find treasure, but they maintained their claim to the Borderlands, because these regions served as buffers between Spain's more settled colonies and the British colonies. To defend their territorial claims, Spanish colonial authorities established settlements in the Borderlands. These communities did not grow up haphazardly, and they did not consist of far-flung individual homesteads. They were planned and organized, in keeping with an official policy of building colonial towns.

Life in Spain was organized around the town, and the colonial authorities reproduced the social and political structures of Spanish town life in the Americas. They did so by following a set of laws that governed how settlements should be organized.

According to these regulations, a community was defined as a *pueblo* (village or town), a *villa* (small city), or a *ciudad* (city). Each community was supposed to include a water source, a forest or stand of trees, and a tract of property considered the king's land, all of which could be used by the whole community. The town or city would be organized around a central square called a plaza. The major public buildings, such as the church or chapel and the government offices, would face this plaza.

Each household of settlers would receive two pieces of land. The *solar* was a lot for building a house in town, while the *suertes* was a section of the gardens, farms, and pastures outside the town. Settlers

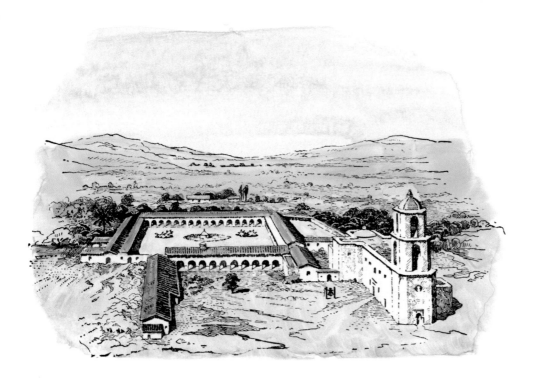

A complex set of regulations governed the organizing and building of Spanish outposts in the Americas. Such Spanish settlements were almost always built around a central square or plaza.

would not live on the land they farmed—they would live in town and go out to work their land.

Settlement did not always follow these regulations to the letter. When moving into new territory, far from existing Spanish communities, officials sometimes found it hard to make settlers obey certain regulations, such as the order to line up the streets of a new town with the direction of the winds, or the instruction to leave Native American towns alone. Occasionally, instead of building a new town, the Spanish settlers simply conquered and occupied a Native American pueblo.

The earliest settlements in the Borderlands were primarily forts. Later, three different kinds of communities developed. The pueblo was a town for settlers, the mission was a center for missionaries who came to Christianize the Indians, and the presidio was a garrison for soldiers. The Spanish settlements in the Borderlands generally combined two or all three of these communities. St. Augustine, in Florida, and Santa Fe, in New Mexico, were two of the most important of these settlements.

The Castillo San Marcos, the sturdy fort that protected the harbor at St. Augustine, Florida, was one of the largest Spanish-built structures in what is now the United States.

St. Augustine was founded in 1565, making it the oldest continuously occupied European city in North America. In its very first form, the settlement was simply a defensive ditch around an Indian council house that the Spanish had taken over. Later, the Spanish chose a better location, with a harbor and a peninsula for a fort. They began building permanent structures, including the Castillo San Marco, the fort that guarded the harbor. Eventually this fort, now a historical site in St. Augustine, became a massive stone and mortar structure with cannon mounted on its battlements and its outer walls ringed with ditches.

The town was never large, and it was never self-supporting. St. Augustine was mainly a presidio, a military garrison kept alive by supplies from the government, that also was associated with several nearby missions. St. Augustine's population numbered about 300 in the 1580s. By 1763, when Britain acquired Florida through a treaty, the settlement had developed into a small town, and the population

This eighteenth-century church was built by the Spanish in Las Trampas, a mountain village in New Mexico.

had increased to about 1,300. Several hundred of the inhabitants were African Americans, some enslaved and some free (Spain had declared that slaves who fled to Florida from the British colonies would be freed if they became Roman Catholics). St. Augustine also had a population of *mestizos*, or people of mixed Spanish and Indian blood.

The first Spanish community west of the Mississippi River was the Villa de Santa Fe, founded in 1608 by Juan Martinez de Montoya, who had become the governor of the province of New Mexico the year before. Martinez believed that the best way for Spain to make use of New Mexico was to establish settler communities and ranches and to carry on a trade in salt and hides with the other Spanish colonies, rather than to keep fighting the Indians and searching for precious metals. His views were unpopular with some of the leading men of the colony, however, so he served as governor for less than a year. The next governor, Pedro de Peralta, sometimes has been given credit for founding Santa Fe, but he simply continued what Martinez had started.

The Pueblo Revolt was a Native American uprising that took Santa Fe out of Spanish hands between 1680 and 1692. During that time, nearly all records of the city's early years were destroyed. Historians do know, however, that Santa Fe's population in 1620 was about 100 people. Despite its small size, Santa Fe had a governor's palace on the north side of the plaza and a church on the east side. The town grew slowly, but in time, as Martinez had hoped, it became the capital of a province of ranchers and farmers.

Building Communities in New France

France's first North American colony was in the valley of the St. Lawrence River, and its first lasting settlement was Quebec. In 1608 Samuel de Champlain established a trading post there, on a hill overlooking the river.

Seventy years earlier, French explorer Jacques Cartier had visited the area and found it inhabited by Native Americans. When Champlain arrived, the natives were gone, although the Algonquin and Montagnais peoples lived not far away. Historians think that the Native Americans of Quebec either had died of diseases introduced by Cartier and his men, or they had been defeated in a war with other Indian groups.

The next stage in Quebec's development came in 1615, when missionaries arrived at the trading post to begin the work of Christianizing the Native Americans. Twelve years later the French crown created the Company of New France to turn the isolated trading post

and mission into a true colony, with permanent settlers. At the time the population of Quebec was seventy-two people. By 1663 it had grown to 550. In that year the crown took control of Quebec away from the company and placed it under a military governor. Quebec became not just the largest community in New France but its administrative center as well. By that time the town had a walled fort, a church, a convent for the education of European and Native American girls, and a hospital.

In the decades that followed, Quebec's population slowly rose. In

Founded by explorer Samuel de Champlain, the city of Quebec, with its fort overlooking the St. Lawrence River, was France's first permanent foothold in North America.

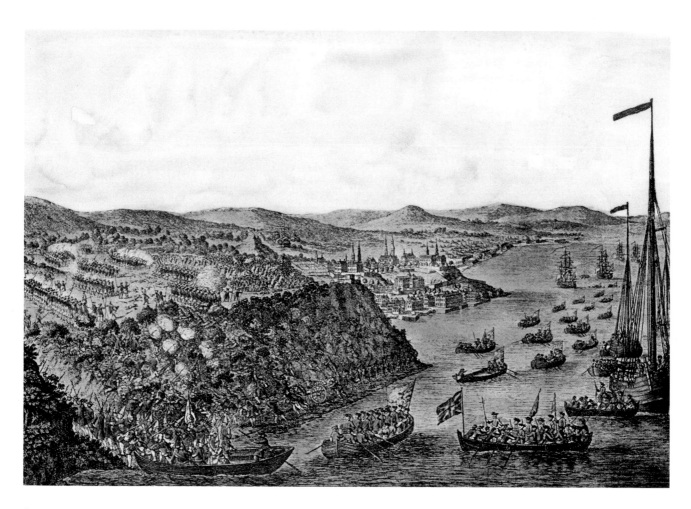

During the French and Indian War, the British attacked Quebec in 1759. The attack was successful, and Canada became a British territory.

1744, the city had 5,200 inhabitants. This population was strongly stratified, or divided into layers and groups that rarely mixed with one another. Military men, members of the religious community, merchants, craftspeople, and servants and laborers existed in what amounted to separate communities. Even at church or during public events, the various segments of the population tended not to mingle. There was considerable concern for maintaining one's proper "place" in life and the community. This contrasted with the more independent ways of life followed by the fur trappers, traders, and canoemen who

The King's Daughters ✆

Marriage was something of a problem in early Quebec. For most of the city's colonial history, men greatly outnumbered women. In the 1660s and 1670s, in the hope of encouraging marriage so that there would be more stable households in the colony, the crown sent 800 or so young women to Quebec. They were called *filles du roi* (daughters of the king), because they were sponsored by King Louis XIV. His agents selected them, and he granted them dowries, or gifts of cash and household goods, with which to start their marriages.

Most of the filles du roi were young ladies who had been orphaned or separated from their families. Marie-Claude Chamois was typical. Although she was one of four children born into a moderately prosperous Paris family, she had run away from home to escape abuse, and she was considered abandoned by her family. A priest placed her in a hospital that sheltered abandoned women. There an agent of the king selected her as a fille du roi. Her attitude toward this life-changing event comes through in a statement preserved in an archive:

> *I was chosen to join a number of others who had to cross to America, and I would have rather renounced my homeland and take a perilous voyage to the New World than beg my mother's help. I resigned myself to silence in an alien land, with neither friends, assistance nor parents, condemned to a perpetual exile.*

The filles du roi were not forced to marry in Quebec, but there was strong encouragement for them to do so, because life in the colony as an unmarried woman was socially and economically difficult. Chamois, who arrived in Quebec in 1670 at the age of fourteen, married a colonist named François Frigon, with whom she had seven children. From the point of view of colonial population policy, hers was a success story.

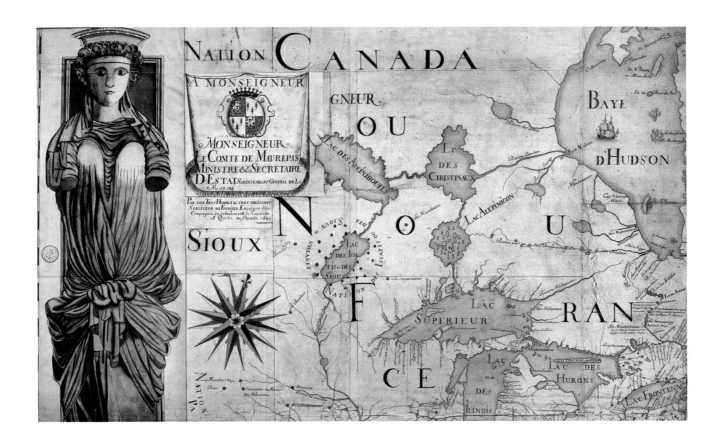

A map of New France, made around 1699, shows the Great Lakes. By following the St. Lawrence River, French explorers and missionaries had reached the lakes and, beyond them, the headwaters of the Mississippi River.

traveled the forests, often living among the Native Americans and marrying Indian women.

Just as Quebec society was divided into levels or categories, each with a different status, the city itself was divided. There was Upper Quebec, the hilltop site of Champlain's original outpost. This part of the city was heavily fortified with stone walls and protected by guns. Most of the religious institutions, as well as the government and military buildings, were located in Upper Quebec. Lower Quebec, which sprawled along the river bank below the hill, was a mass of tall, narrow houses, warehouses, workshops, and businesses facing the harbor.

Quebec fell victim to the conflict between France and Great Britain that flared up again and again during the colonial period, in both Europe and the colonies. The British attacked Quebec unsuccessfully in 1690 and again in 1711.

Then, in 1759, during the French and Indian War, a British force again besieged Quebec. This time the attack succeeded. After firing shells at the city for two months, the British climbed the cliffs and met the French army on a plain behind the walls of Upper Quebec. Although the commanding generals of both sides were killed, the result of the battle was a victory for the British. The French tried to retake the city in 1760, but the British remained in control. The surrender of Quebec marked the end of French North America, even though the colony did not officially pass to British control until three years later, when the two nations signed the Treaty of Paris.

The Treaty of Paris gave Spain ownership of another French colonial city, one that was also located on a river. But the two cities could hardly have been more different. Quebec, perched on its cliff, had cold northern weather and a population that was almost entirely French, Native American, or a mix of the two. Far to the south, just 125 miles (200 kilometers) north of the place where the Mississippi flows into the Gulf of Mexico, was the city of New Orleans. Built on flatlands in a subtropical climate, New Orleans was ethnically and racially diverse.

New Orleans was founded in 1718 as the capital of Louisiana, a French colony along the Mississippi. It served as the main port, administrative center, and largest town of the colony. New Orleans was a planned city. Designed by military engineers, it was laid out as a grid, with a broad avenue and central plaza on the riverfront and neat square blocks of housing lots. New Orleans did not extend much beyond this original section, now called the French Quarter, until the nineteenth century.

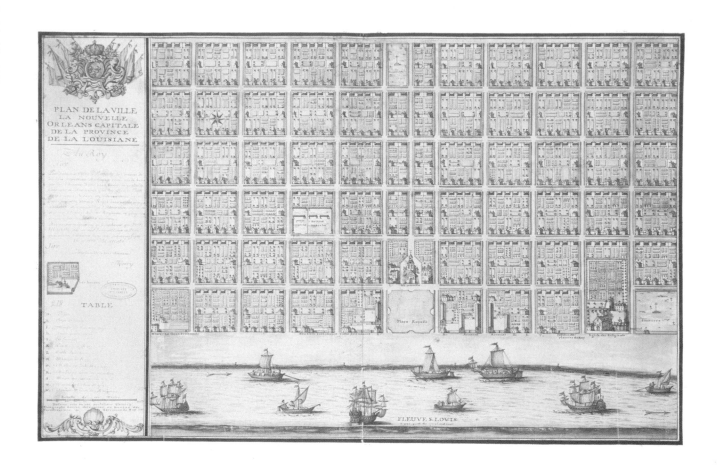

The grid pattern of colonial New Orleans reflects the efficient, straightforward plan of the military engineers who designed the city. The original street plan survives in the French Quarter, the oldest part of New Orleans.

Despite its tidy city plan, New Orleans—and Louisiana in general—was not attractive to settlers. The ground was so swampy that the dead had to be housed aboveground. The summer heat and humidity were oppressive, and diseases such as malaria and dysentery took a heavy toll. In addition, food was always in short supply, as crops were destroyed by floods, storms, and summer droughts.

"Death and disease are disrupting all operations," wrote Jean Baptiste le Moyne, Sieur de Bienville, one of the colony's founders, in 1721, "and, if the famine does not end, all is lost." Ten years later, after about two-thirds of Louisiana's 5,400 European settlers had died, another colonial official penned the pessimistic words, "Little by little, the colony is destroying itself."

New Orleans survived, however. By the 1740s the colony was beginning to produce enough food to feed itself. Although Louisiana never made a profit for the company that first operated it or for the French crown, it did develop a trade in deerskins with the Native Americans, and New Orleans grew into a commercial center.

The city's population was made up of colonists from France (including many convicts sent there by the French government), a group of German Catholics who had emigrated to Catholic Louisiana to escape religious persecution, some Native Americans, and thousands of black slaves, most of them from West Africa. In time, racial intermarriage created a mixed-blood population, the foundation of a distinctive multiethnic culture that remains characteristic of New Orleans today.

With its wide, straight streets and trees planted among brick buildings, Philadelphia was recognized throughout Europe, as well as in the American colonies, as a model of city planning.

CHAPTER FIVE ❧
Urban Life in Early America

CITY DWELLERS WERE A SMALL MINORITY OF THE colonial population. Out of every 100 people in the British colonies in the eighteenth century, only five lived in a city or town with a population larger than 2,500. Yet the importance and influence of cities far outweighed the fact that only 5 percent of the colonists lived in them.

People and goods entered the colonies through the port cities, but so did other things, such as styles and ideas. From the latest fashion in ladies' ribbons and men's shoes to the thoughts of European philosophers on questions of liberty and proper government, cities were points of entry for goods, trends, and concepts that shaped colonial life.

Many significant developments in economics, the arts, and politics started in the cities and spread outward. The shift from a barter economy to a cash economy, in which people paid for goods with money or credit rather than with other goods, happened first in the cities. So did the shift from small, individual workshops to larger commercial crafts operations and, eventually, the first factories. Perhaps most important, colonial cities were the birthplace of political unrest and revolution.

Economic Life

One of the first and most important roles of a city is as a place where people can exchange what they have produced or earned for what they need. The point of exchange was the market, held at a time and place determined by the officials of the colony or community.

The colonies' first market was established in Boston in 1633, just a few years after the Puritans began settling the colony. It was held on Thursdays and drew people from the outlying villages and farms, as well as from all parts of the city. For the first twenty-five years, Boston's market was held outdoors, on King Street. After a town building was constructed, the market moved indoors.

New Amsterdam also had a street market, held every Saturday. By 1662, the city was big and busy enough to hold market day twice a week, on Tuesdays and Saturdays. After the English took over the city in 1664, they constructed a market building. Most other colonial cities and towns had regularly scheduled markets. In addition, some of them had larger market events called fairs, held once or twice a year, that drew people from greater distances.

As centers of trade, colonial cities witnessed a steady flow of outbound goods such as tobacco, rice, wheat, timber and other forestry products, furs and skins, meat, fish, and rum and molasses. The cities were also distribution points for imported goods, including cloth, paper, glass, metal tools, wine, coffee, tea, sugar, spices—and slaves.

The key figures in trade were the merchants, who were more than just buyers and sellers. Merchants also acted as moneylenders before there were banks, as shipbuilders (many merchants owned their own vessels or even fleets), and as land developers. The economic influence of the merchants was great, because they were also the employers of large numbers of sailors and of workers who made such items as barrels and wagons.

Successful merchants in America filled social roles similar to those of aristocrats in Europe. The merchants were the leading citizens in their communities. They wielded considerable political power and also contributed large sums to civic improvements such as schools, libraries, and hospitals.

Skilled crafts workers—also known as artisans, tradespeople, and mechanics—formed another important segment of the urban population. In most cities and towns, half to two-thirds of the taxpaying heads of households were artisans.

Within the artisan population, people held status based on both their level of experience and their particular trade. Master craftsmen, with long experience, had more status than did journeymen, who had learned a trade but not yet reached master status. Journeymen, in turn, outranked apprentices, young people who were working to learn the trade. The trades had their own status ranking, with shoemakers, tailors, and barrel makers at the bottom and carpenters, shipbuilders,

A vital link in the economic life of Philadelphia, and all colonial cities, was porterage, or moving goods from place to place. Whether in a horse-drawn cart, in a wheelbarrow, or on their own strong shoulders, porters moved goods in and out of the centers of trade.

bricklayers, and painters in the middle. At the top were goldsmiths, silversmiths, and makers of musical and scientific instruments.

Below the artisans in social standing were the lower classes. These included sailors, servants, and slaves, as well as unskilled laborers, such as the porters and stevedores who carried loads, and tenant farmers, who worked on agricultural lands owned by other people.

The extremes of wealth and poverty were most visible in colonial cities. The urban centers offered the opportunity for an artisan or small trader to accumulate both status and property. Benjamin Franklin, who rose from an apprentice printer to one of the colonies' most honored and successful businessmen, is a famous example of someone who climbed up the social ladder.

Another example is Thomas Hancock, a minister's son who became a bookseller with a tiny shop in Boston. In Hancock's case, marriage opened the door to social advancement—he married a rich merchant's daughter. Soon Hancock was investing in ships that, among other things, smuggled tea to the colonies. He made a fortune, built a mansion in Boston's fancy Beacon Hill neighborhood, and developed connections with the

An Ounce of Fire Prevention ❧

Benjamin Franklin once had a narrow escape from a house fire. Later in life, Franklin played a key role in organizing Philadelphia's first firefighting companies as well as a fire insurance company called the Philadelphia Contributorship. Franklin also used his newspaper, the *Gazette,* to warn people about the dangers of fire. Here, with typical good humor and an old proverb, he cautions readers to be especially careful when carrying hot coals around the house:

In the first Place, as an Ounce of Prevention is worth a Pound of Cure, I would advise 'em to take care how they suffer living Coals in a full Shovel, to be carried out of one Room into another, or up or down Stairs, unless in a Warmingpan shut; for Scraps of Fire may fall into Chinks and make no Appearance until Midnight; when your Stairs being in Flames, you may be forced, (as I once was) to leap out of your Windows, and hazard your Necks to avoid being oven-roasted.

colony's governor, who gave Hancock highly profitable military contracts to supply British forces in the Caribbean and Canada during wars between Britain and its enemies. Bostonians marveled at Hancock's display of wealth when, in 1748, he imported a four-horse carriage lined with scarlet cloth from London. The fortune made by Thomas Hancock eventually funded the political career of his grandson, John Hancock, one of the Founding Fathers of the United States.

But while mansions rose and carriages rolled along colonial city streets, poverty stalked them, too.

The wars that made fortunes for Hancock and other merchants also killed many colonists who served as soldiers and sailors. Their widows and orphans were often left without financial resources and had to turn to the community for help. City dwellers who did not own property could find themselves among the poor if they lost their jobs. So could disabled war veterans, immigrants who could not find work, and crippled or elderly people without families to support them.

Benjamin Franklin was in many ways a typical, successful, urban, colonial businessman. Not only did Franklin's profession as a printer require a city setting, he relished urban life and contributed time and money to civic causes, including a university and library in Philadelphia.

Churches provided some aid to members of their congregations who fell on hard times, but the main burden of caring for the poor fell on civic governments. To deal with the rising number of homeless people and beggars, cities raised funds through poor relief taxes and built workhouses.

During the eighteenth century, the cost of land in cities and towns rose much faster than the earnings of a typical artisan or laborer. This meant that workers found it increasingly hard to buy homes. More and more of them had to rent living quarters from landlords. In 1700, about 30 percent of urban households lived in rented quarters, but by the end of the century, 80 percent of city dwellers were renters.

The combination of rising real estate prices and lagging wages brought a fundamental change to America's colonial cities. Originally, towns and cities had been made up of neighborhoods that contained a mixture of social classes. People lived where they worked, or close to their place of work. As time went on, however, the cities became divided into zones. The rich were concentrated in the center of town, the middle class in a ring outside the center, and the lower classes in the newest and least expensive residences on the outer fringe of the community.

Social and Cultural Life

For almost everyone in the American colonies, whether they lived in cities, towns, or the countryside, social life revolved around two places: the church and the tavern. Townspeople simply had more churches and taverns to choose from, and they could visit them more easily and more often.

Taverns were more than just places to eat and drink. They were gathering places where people (mostly men, although women did sometimes go to taverns) exchanged news and gossip. Because newspapers or handbills (printed notices) were often available at taverns for the public to read, the taverns were a key part of the colonies' information network. A newcomer to a town or city usually would seek out a tavern, where he might be able to rent a room and find leads on

a job or a place to live. In rural areas, mail for farm households was often delivered to village taverns, to be picked up on the farmer's next visit. In cities, coffeehouses served some of the same purposes as did taverns, acting as settings for social gatherings and political meetings.

The cultural life of the colonies was concentrated in the cities. Schools, libraries, colleges, and theaters appeared in cities and towns. Another significant aspect of urban colonial culture was printing, which began in the colonies in 1638, when the first North American printing press went into business near Cambridge, Massachusetts. Boston acquired its first press in 1674. Philadelphia followed in 1685. By 1700, six printing presses were operating in the colonies.

The presses produced copies of European books for distribution in the colonies. They also printed original American works, such as the writings of the Massachusetts preacher Cotton Mather. At first, most of the printed materials were religious or educational in nature.

Weekly newsletters were becoming popular in England and other parts of Europe, and as early as 1690 a colonist tried to start one. He

Paul Revere, a hero of the Revolutionary War, made this illustration of Harvard College in 1737. By that time, Harvard, the first college in what is now the United States, was more than a century old.

Tale of a Toilet ❧

A highway project begun in 1991, designed to improve traffic flow through Boston, brought to light fragments of the city's colonial past. Known informally as the Big Dig, the project involved moving a highway that ran through the city into a new underground tunnel. The city set aside money for archaeological research in the areas where digging would take place. The idea was to find and preserve any important relics of the past before they were lost forever, destroyed or covered up by the Big Dig.

Urban archaeologists working on the project made some interesting discoveries. One of the most fascinating finds was made under a parking lot in downtown Boston. There, in what was once a small yard, investigators found the remains of a seventeenth-century privy, or outdoor toilet—a "three-seater," according to the project archaeologist. By checking old records, they learned that the property had belonged to a woman with a history of bad luck where husbands were concerned.

Katherine Nanny's first husband died in 1663. The widow Nanny was left with a son, a daughter, and some property: a house, a warehouse, and a wharf. She married a man named Edward Naylor and had two more daughters. In 1671 she separated from her second husband, who ran off to New Hampshire with a servant girl. Katherine Nanny Naylor and her children remained in the house. Their brick-lined privy remained in use until 1708, when it was sealed.

Colonial privies were nothing like modern plumbing. They were deep holes or trenches with benches over them for sitting. In addition to using them as toilets, people often threw garbage or trash into them. For this reason, an archaeologist can sometimes learn a lot by analyzing the contents of an old privy. Katherine Nanny Naylor's privy tells us something about how she and her family lived. It also raises some questions.

Researchers who studied the contents of the privy found the eggs of two different kinds of parasites that live in human intestines. Such parasites were not uncommon in colonial times. They could be spread in dirt, human or animal waste, or infected food. The privy also contained remains of insects and plant materials that indicate the privy was located close to a pond, a mature forest, and some kind of farm building. The privy contained a lot of pollen from grain, which made some investigators think that the household got rid of spoiled or worthless grain by throwing it into the privy.

The family that used the privy had enough money for fine clothing. The archaeologists found more than 150 scraps of silk and woolen cloth, including costly fabrics with stylish trims such as silk ribbons. Five shoes made of high-quality goatskin leather were also found. Three were children's shoes, one would have fitted a young adult, and one was a high-heeled man's shoe. Either the family dressed well, or at some point they threw away their fancy items because of the Puritan colony's laws against showy clothing. Another possibility is that Katherine Nanny Naylor angrily dumped her husband's best clothes into the privy—he wrote to her after he ran off, asking her to send his things and complaining that he had nothing to wear.

The privy also contained a huge number of seeds and pits from fruits, nuts, and spices. More than a quarter of a million of these objects were found, far more than would be normal for a household. Most of them were cherry and plum pits. Archaeologists and historians are not sure what they mean, but some have suggested that Katherine Nanny Naylor might have had a home business making fruit preserves, pies, or possibly cherry bounce, an alcoholic drink that was popular in the colonies.

One of the most striking objects found in the privy went into it in the late seventeenth century, not long before it was filled in. That object is now housed in Boston's Commonwealth Museum, where it is labeled "North America's Oldest Bowling Ball." It is a large, slightly flattened wooden ball with a hole into which lead could be added for extra weight. The ball was once used to play the game that the colonists called "lawne bowles," a form of outdoor bowling. The Puritans disapproved of bowling, because it wasted time and led to the drinking of beer and wine. Massachusetts still had laws against bowling in the late seventeenth century, although the colonists sometimes ignored the laws.

Was the bowling ball in Katherine Nanny Naylor's privy thrown away deliberately, as a symbol of forbidden pleasures? Or did it fall into the privy by accident? Boston's colonial archives can tell us about Katherine Nanny Naylor's troubled marriages, but they do not solve the mystery of the bowling ball in the toilet.

The first manufacturing ventures in the colonies were located in or close to cities. An operation such as this ironworks would most likely have been situated on the edge of town because of the danger of fire.

was a Boston printer named Benjamin Harris. His paper, called *Publick Occurrences*, was promptly crushed by the Massachusetts authorities, who considered it too critical of the government. Perhaps the officials who closed down Harris's paper foresaw the role that newspapers would play in firing up public opinion during the years leading up to the American Revolution.

The first successful attempt at publishing a colonial newspaper came in 1704, with the *Boston News-Letter*. From that time on, one of the most influential functions of print shops was the production of handbills, circulars (announcements or letters meant to be read by the public and passed from hand to hand), and newspapers. By 1775, on the eve of the Revolution, there were forty-eight newspapers in the British colonies.

By keeping colonists informed of events during that turbulent time, the newspapers contributed to the political discussion, debate, and unrest. So did publications such as Thomas Paine's 1776 pamphlet *Common Sense*. Printed in Philadelphia and distributed widely throughout the colonies, Paine's fiery call for the colonies to cut their ties with Great Britain was a bestseller at the close of the colonial era.

Political Life

To many people, political life in the American colonies means the growth of the revolutionary spirit. In reality, American cities were hotbeds of many kinds of political thought and activism throughout the colonial period.

Some political actions had to do with economics and work. Artisans and workers went on strike to demand better conditions, and sometimes the government got involved. In New York City in the late seventeenth century, for example, workers in the transport industry—the porters who carried loads and the carters, or wagoners, who drove wagons—went on strike for higher pay. Colonial officials took them to court for not "Doing their Dutyes."

Riots could break out when times got too hard, as Bostonians discovered in 1713, when a food shortage gripped the city. Town officials warned the colonial government that high prices and scarce provisions could cause trouble. Citizens—including many women, who took a keen interest in food prices, because they were the ones responsible for feeding their families—attacked the ships and ware-

Peddlers offered tea water from a barrel they drove through the city streets. In rural areas, traveling peddlers supplied goods that people could not make for themselves, such as needles and medicines. Urban and rural peddlers also shared other desirable commodities: news, rumors, and gossip.

Burial Hill, in Plymouth, Massachusetts, is the oldest surviving colonial cemetery. Cemeteries, churches, town halls, taverns, shops, markets, and other civic and private institutions knitted together the fabric of community life in colonial America.

houses of a merchant who was selling grain in the Caribbean, because it was more profitable than selling it at home. When the lieutenant governor tried to stop the riot, the rioters shot him. Seventeen years later, in another Boston riot, people tore down the public market as a protest against merchants' high prices.

During the 1760s and 1770s, as the relationship between Great Britain and its North American colonies worsened, the colonies felt growing frustration and economic stress. It was in the cities that this stress took the form of political action, such as the Boston Tea Party and other riots that protested British tax policies. And it was in the coffeehouses, taverns, and pamphlets of the cities that colonists aired their political complaints, shared their ideas about government, and debated the course of action that would lead to the Revolutionary War and American independence.

Timeline ❧

1565	Spain establishes St. Augustine, Florida, the oldest continuously lived-in city in the present-day United States.
1584-1586	England tries to establish a colony at Roanoke, Virginia.
1607	England establishes its first permanent American colony at Jamestown, Virginia.
1608	Samuel de Champlain founds the French colony of Quebec in Canada. Juan Martinez de Montoya of Spain founds Santa Fe, New Mexico.
1620	English Puritans known as Pilgrims settle at Plymouth, Massachusetts.
1624	Families begin to settle in the Dutch colony of New Netherland.
1630	Puritans begin settlement of the Massachusetts Bay Colony.
1636	Harvard College is founded in Massachusetts.
1664	Dutch-controlled New Amsterdam becomes the English city of New York.
1670	Charles Town (later Charleston) is founded in the Carolinas.
1676	Angry colonists led by Nathaniel Bacon burn Jamestown.
1680-1692	A Native American uprising called the Pueblo Revolt takes Santa Fe out of Spanish control.
1681	Englishman William Penn receives a royal charter to found Pennsylvania.
1682	The French claim the Mississippi River valley.
1689	Jacob Leisler tries to restore Dutch leadership in New York, but fails.
1699	Williamsburg becomes the capital of the Virginia colony.
1700	The population of the English North American colonies is about 250,000.
1713	Britain gains control of Nova Scotia, home to some French settlers.
1718	New Orleans is founded by the French.
1733	Savannah, Georgia, is founded.
1739	A slave uprising called the Stono Rebellion shakes Charles Town.
1756-1763	The French and Indian War brings fighting between French and British colonists.
1763	The Treaty of Paris gives French Canada to Great Britain and New Orleans to Spain.
1770-1792	New Bern, founded in 1710, is the capital of North Carolina.
1775	The population of British North America is 2.5 million on the eve of the American Revolution.

Glossary ∾

archaeologist	Scientist who studies past cultures and civilizations, usually by examining physical traces such as ruins and objects left behind.
civic	Having to do with the government or public life of a city or town.
colony	Territory that a state or nation claims outside its own borders.
conquistador	Spanish military explorer who participated in the exploration and conquest of the Americas.
courtier	Member of a king's or queen's court.
emigrant	Someone who leaves his or her homeland to live in another country.
geologist	Scientist who studies the physical structure of the earth, past and present.
heterogeneous	Containing elements that are different or varied.
homogeneous	Containing elements that are the same or similar.
Huguenots	French Protestants.
missionary	Someone who works to convert people to a new religion.
New World	European term for the Americas.
peninsula	Arm of land that sticks out into a body of water.
presidio	Garrison, or residence for soldiers, in the Spanish colonies.
pueblo	Village or town. Used in the Southwest to refer to both Native American and Spanish communities.
Puritan	A Protestant in sixteenth- or seventeenth-century England who wanted to purify, or reform, the church.
Quaker	Member of the Christian religion known as the Society of Friends; also called Friend.
rural	Having to do with the countryside.
seafaring	Traveling by sea. This term can describe a people or nation that makes effective use of ships or boats.
Spanish Borderlands	Parts of the Spanish North American territories that were north of the Mexican colony.
urban	Having to do with cities or towns.

Primary Source List ⁊

Chapter 1 **pp. 20-21** Thomas Morton, "Description of the Indians in New England," from *New English Canaan,* 1637. Available online at http://www.swarthmore.edu/SocSci/bdorsey1/41docs/08-mor.html.

Chapter 2 **p. 30** *South Carolina Gazette* quoted in David S. Shields, "Mean Streets, Mannered Streets: Charleston," in "Early Cities of the Americas," special issue, *Common-Place: The Interactive Journal of Early American Life* 3, no. 4 (July 2003). Sponsored by the American Antiquarian Society and Gilder Lehrman Institute of American History. Available online at http://www.common-place.org/vol-03/no-04/charleston/.

p. 38 Boston officials on the poor quoted in Howard Zinn, *A People's History of the United States,* p. 20. New York: HarperCollins, 2003.

p. 43 Sarah Kemble Knight, "The Journal of Madam Knight." In *The Puritans,* edited by Perry Miller and Thomas H. Johnson. New York: American Book Company, 1938. Available online in the Early Americas Digital Archives at http://www.mith2.umd.edu/eada/html/display.php?docs=knight_journal.xml&action=show.

p. 51 William Penn quoted in Rebecca Stefoff, *William Penn.* Philadelphia: Chelsea House, 1998.

Chapter 3 **p. 60** Michel Guillaume Jean de Crèvecoeur, *Letters from an American Farmer,* Letter I. Online at http://xroads.virginia.edu/~hyper/CREV/letter01.html.

Chapter 4 **p. 73** Marie-Claude Chamois quoted in "Adventurers and Mystics: The Future of New France," Canadian Broadcasting Corporation. Online at http://history.cbc.ca/history/?MIval=EpContent.html&lang=E&series_id=1&episode_id=2&chapter_id=7&page_id=6.

pp. 76-77 New Orleans colonial officials quoted in Alan Taylor, *American Colonies,* p. 385. New York: Viking, 2001.

Chapter 5 **p. 82** Benjamin Franklin's Gazette quoted in "The Philadelphia Contributorship." Online at http://www.ushistory.org/tour/tour_contrib.htm.

For More Information ✑

The books and Web sites listed below contain information about the cities and towns of North America. Most of the books were written especially for young adults. The others will not be too difficult for most young readers. The Web site addresses were accurate when this book was written, but remember that sites and their addresses change frequently. Your librarian can help you find additional resources.

Books

Ciment, James, ed. *Colonial America: An Encyclopedia of Social, Political, Cultural, and Economic History.* Armonk, NY: M.E. Sharpe, 2006.

Cooke, Jacob E., and Milton M. Klein, eds. *North America in Colonial Times: An Encyclopedia for Students.* New York: Scribner, 1998.

Dean, Ruth, and Melissa Thomson. *Life in the American Colonies.* San Diego, CA: Lucent, 1999.

Fisher, Leonard Everett. *Colonial Craftsmen: The Architects.* 1999. New York: Benchmark, 2000.

Hakim, Joy. *Making Thirteen Colonies.* 2nd ed. New York: Oxford University Press, 1999.

Middleton, Richard. *Colonial America: A History.* 2nd ed. Oxford, UK: Blackwell, 1996.

Rossi, Ann. *Cultures Collide: Native Americans and Europeans, 1492–1700.* Washington, DC: National Geographic, 2004.

Smith, Carter, ed. *Daily Life: A Sourcebook on Colonial America.* Brookfield, CT: Millbrook, 1991.

Stefoff, Rebecca. *American Voices from Colonial Life.* New York: Benchmark, 2003.

Web Sites

http://www.americanjourneys.org
A digital library of more than 18,000 pages of original documents about the exploration and settlement of North America. This easy-to-use site is maintained by the Wisconsin Historical Society and funded by the U.S. Institute of Museum and Library Services.

http://home.wi.rr.com/rickgardiner/primarysources.htm
The American Colonist's Library is a collection of primary sources—documents that shaped the history of the American colonies. A number of city and town charters are included.

http://www.mith2.umd.edu/eada/
A rich collection of primary sources for the American colonies. Supported by the University of Maryland, the Early Americas Digital Archive is a gateway to online texts of documents written in the Americas, or about them, between 1492 and about 1820.

http://www.civilisations.ca/vmnf/vmnfe.asp
The Virtual Museum of New France includes maps and sections on daily life and education in French North America.

http://www.history.org/History/index.cfml
The Colonial Williamsburg Web site offers an introduction to life in this early American community in Virginia.

http://falcon.jmu.edu/~ramseyil/colonial.htm
Colonial America 1600–1775 offers links to hundreds of articles and educational Web sites about many aspects of life in the North American colonies.

Index

Note: Page numbers in italics refer to pictures and maps.